THINK!

THINK!

Change
Your
Story...
Change
Your Life.

KEVIN L. KING

THINK! Change Your Story, Change Your Life
By Kevin L. King
Published by Transformation Press
Denver, CO

Second Edition ©2016
First edition copyright ©2006
Kevin L. King, All rights reserved.

All rights reserved. No part of this book may be used or reproduced in any manner whatsoever without the written permission of the publisher and author, except by a reviewer who may quote passages in a review.

All images, logos, quotes, and trademarks included in this book are subject to use according so trademark and copyright laws of the United States of America.

Library of Congress Control Number: 200690552
King, Kevin L., Author
THINK! Change Your Story, Change Your Life

ISBN-13: 978-0-9787075-0-7

Edited by: Kathryn Gould
Designed by: Nick Zelinger with NZ Graphics

QUANTITY PURCHASES: Schools, companies, professional groups, clubs, and other organizations may qualify for special terms when ordering quantities of this title. For more information, email Transformation Press at Marketing@Transformationpoint.com

Printed in the United States of America.

All rights reserved by Kevin L. King and Transformation Press

↻
To my wife Lisa!
You have always believed in me and have
been in my corner from the time we first met.
It is special to have someone see in you
what you find difficult to see in yourself.

Contents

Preface
13

About the Text
15

Chapter One
The Journey
19

Chapter Two
Consciousness
27

Chapter Three
Alignment
55

Chapter Four
Reinvention
75

Chapter Five
Accountability
105

Chapter Six
Relationship Management
125

Chapter Seven
Reflection
145

Chapter Eight
Implications
161

Bibliography
167

About the Author
171

ACKNOWLEDGMENTS

Thank you to my friends and family who have played important roles in my personal and professional growth. I remain a work of art in process thanks to your feedback and efforts to keep me conscious.

PREFACE

Many of us don't recognize that the only obstacle in the way of our personal and/or professional success waits in the mirror to greet us each morning. We often strive to achieve better results without challenging the thinking that produced our current situation. We don't realize that our internal scripts must be rewritten before new levels of performance can be achieved. Those internal scripts, the cognitive stories that drive our behavior, must first be challenged and aligned with desired results before improvement can be possible. The trick is to gain insight into those cognitive stories, thereby revealing the thinking that leads to poor results.

By recasting our individual stories, we can change our performance. This requires overcoming the inertia created by our self-reinforcing individual stories. It also requires that we accept and master managing who we really are and the motivational needs that drive us. The goal is not to change who we are but to master self-management and our human dynamic. The purpose of this book is to expose you to a new set of practices that can help you in all of these areas.

This book outlines six integrated concepts that assist individuals in achieving better results. These concepts are consciousness, alignment, reinvention, accountability, relationship management, and reflection.

ABOUT THE TEXT

This book is about the whole self and not the divided self. It is about the human dynamic in all aspects of our lives. Putting these concepts into practice can help you personally and professionally in several areas: identifying where you are in your journey and what might be getting in the way of your personal growth, life satisfaction and success; understanding the human dynamics that may be making it unnecessarily difficult for you to achieve the desired results; finding and maintaining your center; and dealing with and accepting others who are at different places in their own growth journeys and who may help or hinder your attempts to grow.

The story in this text is a personal one: it is my own journey from childhood to the present. My hope is that many of you will be able to identify with this journey, or at least the key aspects of it, as you make your way through several metaphorical "Cities" representing steps to greater personal efficacy. Accompanying you will be a "Traveler", whose thoughts and musings will help you as you grapple with the various personal growth opportunities and shifts in perspective that challenge both the Traveler and you to grow beyond current boundaries. There are "Teachers" living in the cities you will pass through. Each one represents real life scholars, schools of thought, or individuals I have met who have challenged my thinking and introduced me to practices that have helped me find my way. Lastly, there are theoretical foundations supporting each discovery I have made.

My baggage, my path, and my journey are all metaphors to help you connect with the theoretical constructs at play. My journey reveals my confrontations with myself and my constant challenge of growing from the inside out. I have often been tempted to project my issues onto others and blame my circumstances for my condition. The challenges I have faced and continue to face are challenges that plague many of us as we journey toward taking ourselves to increasing levels of personal growth and effectiveness.

Each chapter contains a discussion section with an interpretation of the works cited to provide you with a theoretical context and filter to process my experiences along with your own.

This journey is through the never ending landscape of personal development. We humans are much more effective when we are conscious, aligned, continually reinventing ourselves (growing), accountable, present, and reflective. Please accompany me on this journey and commit to "THINK!" about how my journey can help you with your own personal journey. Below are the steps to personal growth outlined in this book:

The City of Consciousness
Understand your needs and then surface and confront your thinking in order to begin the journey to becoming your most effective self.

The City of Alignment
Align your purpose, goals, thinking, practices, passion, and find your authentic self.

The City of Reinvention
As we grow and learn, we will inevitably discover the need to reinvent ourselves and recover from what we did not know or would not acknowledge about ourselves.

The City of Accountability
Accept your responsibilities and continue to develop your character. Hold yourself accountable for the conditions you create.

The City of Relationship Management
Communicating in a way that increases the openness between individuals and within teams, fosters opportunities for knowledge creation, learning, personal growth, and collaboration.

The City of Reflection
Reflection is the pathway to learning and reinvention.

[**T H I N K !**]

CHAPTER ONE

An only child and a loner, I spent most of my childhood living in my own mind. I constructed my own fantasy theme, purposefully designed to protect me from the cruelty of the world and the reality of my circumstances.

My escape from reality was spent watching television and pretending to be someone I was not. One minute I was imagining myself as a gunfighter and the next a racecar driver. I escaped into fantasy as a distraction from my reality, passing most of my time imagining what it would be like to live a different life. In the life portrayed on television everything was possible: mothers nurtured their children, fathers were present and engaged. This was not my existence.

I was just a boy living in an imaginary world until the cruelty of bullies would snap me back into the reality from which I felt I could not escape, consisting of circumstances I could not control. I was sick of the endless taunting and teasing from the other children. I was poor, from a broken home, and my mother was diagnosed as a paranoid schizophrenic. Her drug use did not help the situation either; she was constantly self-medicating to escape the reality of her life. Frankly, my mom was an embarrassment to me. However, this was in the 1960s and early 1970s when our country's approach to mental health issues was much less mature.

It was not until my own son had what was diagnosed as a psychotic break while we were on vacation in Italy that I began to really understand the suffering my mother endured. She was illegally sterilized and had numerous shock treatments to the point that the hair on her temples was permanently lost. I remember visiting her in the state mental institution in Rusk, TX, seeing her walking around like a zombie, and not understanding why she couldn't come home. Again, not until my own son was diagnosed as bipolar did I truly understand why she would not take her medications and end up institutionalized over and over again. I did not understand why she slit her wrists and repeatedly attempted to kill herself.

My early childhood was one tragic episode after another. One day I would be told people were after us, and the next night I would be sitting in the backseat of a car freezing, waiting for my mom and stepdad to get their fix of codeine (syrup as it was called back then).

My fighting and outbursts of anger would eventually get me appointments with the school psychologist. The intervention was to give me red tabs for good behavior each time I was able to control my response to being bullied and teased: bullied because I was considered "soft" and a mama's boy, and teased for being poor and because of my mother's reputation for sleeping around and being a "crazy" person.

This was my life until I moved to live with my dad and stepmother in Midland, MI, when I was thirteen. But I would return to my grandmother's home in Port Arthur, TX, my senior year of high school, and the relationship between my mother and me only got worse. The calls coming in late into the night, the yelling and screaming matches, the sheer embarrassment of not being able to talk about my mother the way others talked about theirs created an empty space in my being and added to my baggage.

Being born into poverty really took its toll. If nothing else, once I recognized that I was poor, I decided that I didn't want to live that way as soon as I was able to make my own choices. As a man, I was willing to do anything to escape the struggle of my early childhood. I knew I did not want to make the mistakes I had seen others make, and I knew I would have to learn how to get out of my own way. Of course, I did make those same mistakes and in many instances I compounded them.

Eventually, I decided that I would leave this all behind and press forward. But I did not know what to expect as I took my first steps toward independence and separation from my past. I had no idea how difficult it would be to unpack my baggage and change my life.

Change can be tough for anyone, and I soon learned that it would be challenging for me too. My only consolation was my interest in discovering what was possible for me. I hoped I would better myself, but I was not yet conscious of my true self or the lifetime of self-discovery I faced. There is a difference between changing who you are and changing how you manage yourself and make choices. I have learned that changing who I am is not possible. However, managing myself and my choices more effectively is definitely achievable and sustainable.

My baggage was my challenge, but I did not understand this at the time. I had carried it so long that I had become unconscious of its existence and how it influenced my perspective. I didn't know what to expect ahead, and I could not foresee the long and winding road of my journey.

Hope was in my heart. As my starting point began to fade in the distance, I began to feel a sense of loss for that which was familiar to me. I did not realize how comfortable I had become with my circumstances. I had a self-reinforcing story. It would have been easy for me to accept my circumstances and settle for a life of complacency and excuses. It would be simple to play the victim. Often I was tempted to just stay home. What sane person would leave a familiar and comfortable place to figure out what was possible instead of accepting things as they were? Then again, what sane person would choose to struggle so? Sometimes I thought I should just stay put and see what tomorrow would offer. But that seemed much too close to the thinking that had kept me from leaving sooner. That routine wasn't changing anything and only increased my complacency. I filtered these thoughts as I escaped into my imaginary world of fantasizing about living like people did on television. I realized how tempting it was to take what seemed to be the easy path, to do nothing or refuse to take accountability for myself, instead of kicking myself in the butt and focusing on what I could do. I didn't know that this was only the beginning of a life filled with attacking my challenges head on, many of which were results of my own bad choices.

For several days I contemplated my pursuit of what was possible for my life. I had many questions. What's missing? What's possible? What will make me happy? Who am I? What in the hell can I do to get out of here? More questions than answers raced through my mind as I sat staring into the television or listening to music. I knew I could only generate answers to my questions based on my own perspective. Something inside of me questioned how I could ever discover what was possible without learning to see multiple sides of my dilemma. I was intent on finding others who could help me navigate my journey, those who could see what I could not.

DISCUSSION

I had to make a choice. I could continue on the path of many of my friends, or I could pick a different route. Regardless, I knew it was time for me to make my own decisions, create my own conditions, and live with the consequences. I needed to escape.

We all are born into circumstances, rich or poor, one or two parent homes, loving or abusive relationships, and these circumstances affect our expectations in life. The stories and scripts we receive from the key influencers in our lives and the experiences we have had continue to affect us throughout our lives, coloring the way we think about and react to others and to the events unfolding around us. And then those thoughts and reactions lead to decisions which shape our future—often to look just like our past.

Consider this: how frequently will the average person be able to successfully set aside his biases in his interactions with others? Even on a good day, a thoughtful, conscious person probably doesn't do this consistently. And when we are stressed or not focusing on what we're doing, we often blindly follow the scripts that we inherited from our influencers without even being aware of it.

How might following those unconscious scripts be affecting our lives? Might they be hindering us professionally? Could they be preventing us from developing relationships that would help us grow, either personally or in our careers? What opportunities have we missed because we were stuck in our old ways of thinking? Chapter Two will dive deeper into how we can become aware of these preformed biases and how we can begin to change them. For now, THINK! about your current circumstances, your hopes and dreams for the future, and what you are willing to do to move from point A to point B.

Reflections

At the conclusion of each chapter you will have the opportunity to answer several primer questions to help you determine how to apply what you have read. The following is a set of questions to help you reflect on why you are reading this book and how it might help you.

Complete the following threads:
1. I am reading this book because...
2. After reading this book I hope to be able to...
3. The author and I are similar in that I...
4. The author and I are different in that I...
5. My circumstances are/were...
6. My baggage is...
7. My journey is toward...
8. The key influencers in my life are and have been...
9. My personality tendencies consist of...
10. The major influencing experiences in my life have been...
11. When I review my own personal "outcomes," my growth and effectiveness are blocked by...
12. I get my motivation from...
13. My friends see me as...
14. The people who don't like me say that I am...
15. The top five areas of my life where I need help are...

"Understand your needs and then surface and confront your thinking in order to begin the journey to becoming your most effective self."

[T H I N K !]

CHAPTER TWO

My journey started in Port Arthur, Texas in 1964. The baggage I was born with consisted of two pieces: one bag filled with my circumstances, things I did not choose and could not control: an environment of poverty, drug addiction and mental illness; the second bag was left empty for me to fill with the conditions that I would inevitably create for myself. My experience has taught me that my journey is as much about living to learn as it is about learning to live.

Growing up, PA was our familiar name for Port Arthur, Texas. Most people have probably heard of it in relationship to hurricane Rita (2005). Get out your map and you will find that it is on the Gulf Coast about 90 miles southeast of Houston, Texas. It is part of the Golden Triangle consisting of Port Arthur, Beaumont, and Orange, TX.

Surprisingly, PA was a great place to grow up. As a child, I thought that everything I experienced there was normal because I did not have an alternative frame of reference. My experience in PA seemed to be the way things were for everyone. I had so much to learn about my biases and assumptions.

Today, I have a different perspective of those experiences, and a much clearer view of how I have spent most of my adult life overcoming the scripts that were blocking my personal growth. I had to overcome my PA mentality, my bias that the rest of the world was much the same as PA. I had to overcome my interpretation of my lived experience and the rules that applied in the environment that shaped the early years of my life.

My baggage was heavy, and I just kept making it heavier. I still find myself stuffing a few bricks in every now and then. That's what happens when you are unaware of the power that your circumstances and your baggage play in life. I may be unusual, but it took several direct encounters with brick walls before I actually became semi-conscious. It is amazing what you learn when you finally decide to think about what you are doing and attempt to understand your patterns of behavior and their sources. It took me a while to understand that my thinking was the only thing I could change. That was difficult because I did not realize the need. I did not realize the drivers behind my emotions and my worldview.

I was born into circumstances that were less than ideal but not the worst case scenario by far. I was born into social, economic, and environmental circumstances. Some circumstances are better than others; at least that is what I learned to believe. Arguably, many of us consider being born poor a greater burden than being born rich. While we carry this assumption, few of us are conscious of its origin. Where does this perception come from?

Is our perception a product of our scripting? Have the stories we have heard through the media, parents, grandparents, siblings, extended family, religious leaders, teachers, or other key influencers in our lives resulted in mental scripts we aren't even aware of? Has our perception grown out of our work experiences, our relationships with others, or other life experiences we've had along the way? How about all of the above? Is the privileged person impacted any less by their influencers or lived experiences?

In addition to our circumstances, we all have internal needs and motivators that make us unique and affect our reactions to the world around us and our perceptions of it. If only it ended there.

Allowing scripts to drive our behavior with the persons we encounter is a subtle form of "profiling." Profiling is not always negative, but it is something that we do often in our everyday lives. In fact, most personality and style assessments put us into boxes that indicate our style or behavioral preferences. These typically align with our internal needs. If we could, we would likely create the world in our own images because that would mean that the world would then cater to our needs.

Once we have a "label" we learn how to best interact with people who have a particular "profile." This is all intended to help us be more effective at interacting with others in order to produce better results. But the other side of profiling, the side that may get in the way of someone's success, consists of the scripts and rules that are subconsciously at play during interactions with others. These scripts and rules are characterized by responses such as, "If they would only do it my way, we would not have these problems," or "You aren't supposed to..." Applied consciously or unconsciously, these biases limit our ability to accomplish goals. The trick is to become aware of one's own biases and assess whether they help or hinder, block or enable.

The following diagram may be useful in determining the origin of your thinking. It reflects the information discussed in this chapter thus far.

SCRIPTING

SCRIPTING ▶

INFLUENCERS	TENDENCIES	EXPERIENCES	OUTCOMES
Parents	Emotional I.Q.	Work	Values
Grandparents	Academic Ability	Social	Beliefs
Siblings	Intellect	Cultural	Biases
Extended Family	Athletic Ability	Academic	Paradigms
Teachers	Personality	Travel	Rules
Social Workers	Social Style	Relational	Phobias
Spiritual Advisors	Curiosity	Familial	Fears
Mentors	Social Skills	Other	Motivations
Friends	Musical Ability		Trust Systems
Television	Drive		Habits
Books	Ambition		Practices
Others			Methods
			Ethics

◀ UNSCRIPTING

In the scripting process the Influencers impart to us stories that we process based upon our own personalities and tendencies. Our scripts are further influenced by our life experiences. Our life experiences culminate and are reflected in how we interact with our world and what we believe at a given point in time. In the unscripting process, we call into question those stories and the resulting scripts to determine their validity and continued relevance. Unfortunately, this often happens too late and sometimes follows some compelling event in our lives that causes us to question who we are. What a painful process to only learn about ourselves when forced to and to reflect only in a time of crisis.

I was not sure of my destiny when I left home to join the Air Force, but I was certain that I didn't want things to be the way they had been. At that time I had a pregnant girlfriend, who became my wife before I left for basic training. While my journey was certain to present obstacles and opportunities, I was sure that anything would be better than being a deadbeat dad or raising my children in poverty. I knew I was not going to get rich in the Air Force, but I knew I could finish my education and that my wife and child would have healthcare coverage. Most importantly, I would be leaving home and standing on my own two feet for the first time in my life. My decision introduced me to new experiences and with those new experiences came challenges to my thinking. But I constantly tried to frame my new experiences in the context of my old ones. This made it difficult for me to broaden my perspective.

Over time, I developed several biases for how I should live my life; those biases helped me to redirect the uncertain toward the certain, to move gray areas into the realm of black or white. As was the case for many people from my past, black and white was safe, clean, unambiguous and left no questions. However, it did not lead to new possibilities. The influencers in my life presented their own biases, many of which I adopted as my own. I never thought to question the biases I encountered during my interactions with them. Thus, I had no idea that my reality and sense of self were distorted by these invisible influences.

For years, my journey presented several nuances that challenged my thinking. Of the people I met along the way, many seemed to be quite self-possessed. Others seemed either intent upon questioning the motives behind my choices or completely determined to turn me in another direction. It seemed simple for me to critique their character and make conclusions about their motives; however, I neglected to question my own character and motives. I failed to see that I, too, was biased. In each of the interactions I experienced with others, I shared my own biases for the way they should pursue their lives. I was articulate and persuasive, so I experienced a great deal of success—many people bought into my perspectives.

Others simply concluded that I must be new to my journey, so they were polite but dismissed my advice. They could see that I was not modeling what I advocated, but I could not. My rules did not appear to apply to me.

On several occasions, I tried to convince fellow journeymen that their approach to navigating their path was not sustainable. Given the nature of the pathway they pursued, this was quite important. They simply listened to my thoughts and nodded politely. This behavior irritated me because I perceived them as being dismissive of my perspective and advice. My demeanor and mannerisms became intense and assertive. Unconsciously, I began to become dogmatic, passionate, and right. In the eyes of others, I was abrupt, empty and conflicted—unconscious and unable to see that I was in my own way. I could not see what others could see in me. I could not see who I was being. I had no insight into the thinking driving my behavior.

Eventually, I reached my City of Consciousness. I realized that I needed to better understand who I was being and why. I began my search for Teachers; people who could help me learn how to understand myself. I was constantly getting in my own way because of my self-reinforcing stories, but I persevered. I thought of it as looking for my temple of Truth. As I sought out my temple, I was greeted by many Teachers. It is amazing how many people are willing to help you when you open yourself up to it.

I quickly learned that I had to improve my ability to articulate what I was seeking. I needed to be able to explain my limited worldview and the journey that had lead me to seek a higher level of consciousness. In essence, I had to make my thinking open, public, and discussable. I had to open myself to having my thinking challenged and scrutinized. I had to make myself vulnerable to judgment and criticism.

At first, I started describing the pursuit of something that was not immediately tangible or even explainable. I was basically asking: "How do I understand and define my personal destiny?" The general response was "How will you know when you have found your destiny?" My response was so immature at first. I simply replied, "I will not be where I started." I had not yet truly gotten my head around what I was really pursuing. But I could clearly articulate what I didn't want.

This eventually led to asking, "Who are you?" This was one of the most intimidating questions I had ever been confronted with at that stage in my life. I felt I needed to have the right answer. My answer eventually became "I am seeking never to return to the circumstances I was born into. I am also seeking to overcome the challenges and conditions I have created for myself along the way." My answer today is generally the same with one major exception. Instead of overcoming challenges and conditions, I spend most of my time trying to make better choices that minimize unnecessary challenges to start with.

The Journey Begins

When the Traveler first arrived in the City of Consciousness, he found to his surprise that it was not densely populated. Seeking a Teacher here, he quickly learned the reason for that: the City of Consciousness is full of mirrors, forcing the inhabitants to constantly evaluate their own choices and behavior. In addition, constructive feedback is the main course of every meal. The Teacher also described a tale of two cities. The other, the City of Unconsciousness, was densely populated. Many preferred this city because there were no mirrors, and constructive feedback was not allowed.

In the City of Unconsciousness people used to conduct

business and dine on the promenade of the city center, doing only what was comfortable and natural for them. They were able to be their natural selves without risk of rejection or ridicule. There was no concern for how one's natural self might be negatively perceived by others or impact others negatively. As they engaged with business partners and friends, they would never notice their own habits and maneuvers. They never worried about how they appeared to others. But over many years, they began to communicate differently; intimate and authentic talks were replaced by superficial conversation that lacked substance and depth.

The Teacher went on to explain that the city's inhabitants were an inwardly beautiful and loving people. Aside from their inward beauty, they made up one of the wealthiest developed cultures in the world. As time continued to pass, they grew in their drive to maintain their wealth and status. Eventually, as the resources to create wealth became scarce and economic power was gradually consolidated into the hands of a few powerful families, conflicts and quarrels ensued. "As a culture, the inhabitants of this beautiful city struggled to reconcile their inward selves with the reality of who they had become once their wealth and status was lost." They were stressed and conflicted. Their old stories of self could not be reconciled with who they were being.

The Teacher went on to tell the Traveler that this conflict began to infect their treatment of one another. They criticized and verbally attacked each other. Their frustration and anger erupted at the least provocation—they were toxic. As these people became more and more guarded, reserved and overly sensitive, the age of political correctness began. That is, people began saying not what they truly thought or felt, but only what was necessary to maintain civility for fear of personal attack. People learned to be inauthentic and passive aggressive. Defensive routines became well engrained.

The once vibrant city eventually lost its appeal and became an unattractive place to live and work, causing the infrastructure and the culture to crumble. Eventually, a small group of people decided that they had had enough. They struck out on their own, deciding to create a new city and a new way of life. In order to save themselves from the social decline they had witnessed in the City of Unconsciousness, a law was passed ordering that mirrors be placed in all public spaces in the new city.

The Traveler interrupted, "These people are descended from those in the City of Unconsciousness? They don't seem at all insensitive or self-absorbed to me."

Not fazed by the interruption, the gracious host sipped from his teacup and continued his story. "Their children reinvented their culture, hoping to avoid their parents' mistakes. They developed a cultural philosophy that would teach people to use their reflections constructively for personal growth and development. Filling the city with mirrors, the succeeding generation determined not to hide from their true selves or the developmental feedback that would help them learn, grow, and thrive. They refused to be in denial about their true natures and to work diligently to become their most effective selves. When they looked into the mirror they were eager to confront themselves and to ask and answer the questions, 'Who am I? What are my needs? Who am I being at this moment? How does who I'm being impact others? What is the thinking that is driving my current behavior? What are my biases?' Their answers, although individual, were the products of all of the interactions they saw themselves having with their friends, families and strangers.

"They could not escape the reality of who they were being in the moment. They could easily see when they were more focused on self than other. They believed that they came to truly know themselves by evaluating their interactions with others. They also discovered a secret that their ancestors had not. Being self-aware was not enough. They also had to interact with the intention of contributing to the greater good of others and their relationships. In other words, they realized that focusing primarily on their own needs once again would lead to self-destruction and the collapse of their society. They created an open and safe environment so that they could feel comfortable sharing their needs and inner thoughts with others. They learned to embrace feedback, even when the feedback indicated that they needed to improve.

"Now, I ask you again, who are you?" The Traveler paused before responding. "I am the person I see in the mirror when I am standing in front of it alone."

"Who do you want to be?"

"I would like to be the person standing in the mirror accompanied by others, seeing myself through not only my eyes but their eyes as well. I would like to have each of us see the same person and know that what we see is true and authentic. But more importantly, I want others to see that I mean them no ill will and that I want to engage with them in understanding and valuing our differences."

Over their meal, the Teacher and Traveler discussed many

things. Eventually, the Teacher introduced the question of truth into their dialogue. In response, the Traveler revealed that he was not certain that man is able to embody truth. He doubted that a human being has the capacity to see another through a lens that is not distorted by personal biases and judgments.

The Teacher was deeply intrigued by this insight. He continued to ask questions of the Traveler.

"What do you know of the essence of truth?"

"The essence of truth is in intent. The intention of a person presenting his truth must be to factually and accurately represent the past, present, or desired future."

"What is the intent of a person when he evaluates the reflection he sees in the mirror?"

"To tell the truth about what he sees."

The Teacher continued. "What can get in the way of this?"

"An intent which may be to make one's self appear better than another or to hide from one's true self."

"How can this be overcome?"

By now, the Traveler noticed the significance of the questioning and became extremely engaged. "By accepting ourselves for where we are in our own journey and seeking to learn from others who are at different stages in their journeys."

"Does this mean that we should accept that each of us still has much to learn and that our journey is just that, our journey? Is it fair to expect others to follow our path, or should we help them to pave their own?"

The Traveler considered this idea for a long moment. "But how can I overcome my need to tell others what they should do?" He began now to recognize some of the previous offenses he had committed against other travelers.

The Teacher inquired. "What do you gain from this telling?"

"I gain nothing. I only want to help fellow travelers along their journeys."

The Teacher again inquired. "Has this helping been for your benefit or theirs?"

The Traveler did not have an immediate response. After reflecting for a while he said, "I want to help others, but now I realize that my biases influence my advice to others, and this can be unintentionally harmful. But I must be responsible for understanding what biases I have and put those on the table when advising others. Better yet, as you have done with me, I should ask them questions that help them to find their own answers."

He continued. "This will be difficult for me because I usually think I already have the answers they need. I must accept that my answers are the answers that work for me. The best gift that I can give to others is to have them truly reflect on their own image by asking questions relevant to the dilemmas they struggle with. I guess I have to accept that I can't give another person what they are missing. Each person must find what he needs for himself. I must accept that, as I continue my journey, I might find that the answers I have for myself change as I learn more from my travels."

The Teacher was silent as the Traveler vocalized his thoughts. He felt both joy and anguish for the Traveler as he watched him work through the answers to his questions. He could see that the Traveler was both freed and burdened by his Consciousness. When he looked into the Traveler's eyes it was as if he could see the scenes he was replaying in his mind of all the times he had advised others based upon where he was in his journey. He had not known what he didn't know.

The Traveler realized how little he truly knew and felt embarrassed by the thought of how ignorant he must have appeared to some of the others he had encountered on his journey. The Teacher felt his pain as he saw tears stream from the Traveler's eyes. "What is it that pains you so, my son?"

The Traveler attempted to regain his composure but could not. He began to sob uncontrollably. It was as if he was decompressing all of his inward anxiety and frustration resulting from his being in conflict with himself. The Teacher could see that the Traveler was experiencing a moment of intense honesty with himself.

A long while passed, and the Traveler managed to compose himself. He told his host, now his coach, that he had been wearing a mask for so long that he had lost his ability to recognize himself. He felt like everything he had known was wrong, that he had to now accept that he too was just a learner on a journey. He did not know how he could exist without knowing.

To this the Teacher responded, "We all are learners, and the greatest gift that we can give ourselves is to accept this truth. To travel our journey as a knower may limit our very ability to find that which we seek or to recognize we are heading toward the wrong destination. My belief is that we must be open to challenging our beliefs and biases so that we can open ourselves up to learning. But you must discover your own truth about these matters."

It had now become very late into the evening, and the Traveler was completely exhausted. He could walk no further, cry no more tears, nor answer more questions. He asked the Teacher if he could stay for the evening, and the Teacher gladly obliged.

The next day, as the Traveler was packing to continue his journey, he heard a slight knock at the door to his quarters. The Teacher was there holding a tray containing a hefty plate of fruit and two cups of tea. Sipping from his cup, the Teacher asked the Traveler whether he recognized the gift he had given himself the prior evening.

The Traveler thought for a moment before responding. "You have given me an abundance of gifts. I have received the gift of questioning and an understanding of truth. I think the gift I have given myself is the gift of Consciousness. You have been my mirror. I have seen myself through your questions, and I believe that I have found a truth about myself that I would not have discovered otherwise."

To this the Teacher said, "Your gift was in letting yourself find your own answers and your own truth. I recognize that I have influenced you, but you must process what we have shared here and apply that which challenges you to be better." The Teacher then handed the Traveler a small mirror. "Here is a small gift to help you on your journey. It will remind you of the need to continue to practice being conscious and not to fall into complacency. Your journey is a noble one. I wish you well. My sister lives in the distant City of Alignment should you find your way there and need to rest."

"What is her name?"

"Her name... is Lorelei. I will notify her that you may be

stopping through, should your journey lead you there. I have enjoyed meeting you, and I have enjoyed our conversations. I hope your journey is better for your visit."

The Traveler thanked the Teacher for his hospitality as he finished packing his bags. As he was doing so, he realized that somehow he needed one less bag. He concluded that nothing was missing, so he asked if he could leave the empty bag with the Teacher, and the Teacher agreed. The Traveler picked up his baggage and chose the path toward the City of Alignment. He turned to speak one last time to the Teacher. "I never learned your name."

"Maxim. I am Maxim."

"And I am..."

"There is no need to name yourself. Along your journey you will discover the need to name many other things. The names and faces of people will fade over time but their impact on your life will likely never be forgotten. I have come to know you without a label. That is enough for me. Blessings on your journey, my friend and brother."

Discussion

Several scholars and practitioners have directly or indirectly addressed the concept of consciousness in their research. The authors that have impacted me the most are Peter Senge, *The Fifth Discipline* (1990), Chris Argyris and Donald Schön, *Theory in Practice* (1974), James Prochaska, *Changing for Good* (1994), Daniel Goleman, Richard Boyatzis, and Annie

McKee, *Primal Leadership* (2002), Howard Gardner, *Changing Minds* (2004), Stephen Brookfield, *Developing Critical Thinkers* (1987), and Nathaniel Branden, *The Psychology of Self-Esteem* (1969) and *The Six Pillars of Self-Esteem* (1994). This list is short because reading their works made my battle with consciousness very real.

My interpretation of their works leads me to conclude that, as human beings, we are challenged by our ability to achieve and maintain awareness of our thinking and how that thinking impacts our experience with the world. If we are not conscious of the fears, values and biases that drive our behavior and actively striving to close the gap between who we say we are and who we actually are, we risk never becoming our most effective selves.

I have had to stand before a mirror and confess, "My name is Kevin King and I am a recovering 'unconsciouholic.' As an unconsciouholic I suffer from chronic lapses in consciousness about who I am being. I have found that my words and actions often do not align. I have tried to change my approach to get the results I seek, but I rarely call into question my expectations. Each day I suffer from unconsciousness about some aspect of my thinking and/or who I am being as I navigate my interactions with others."

Initially, my great challenge was in stating this recognition daily. I practice having this mindset when I have personal or professional interactions with others. I have found that increasing my level of consciousness impacts those interactions.

Another way of looking at consciousness is that it is a pattern developed over time. In other words, if I live my life as a learner, I gain more knowledge and insight about others and myself. Conversely, if I live my life deflecting new information, I don't learn, and I don't grow. Eventually, I develop large, detrimental blinds spots.

The following diagram reflects that living life as a learner is like a helix.

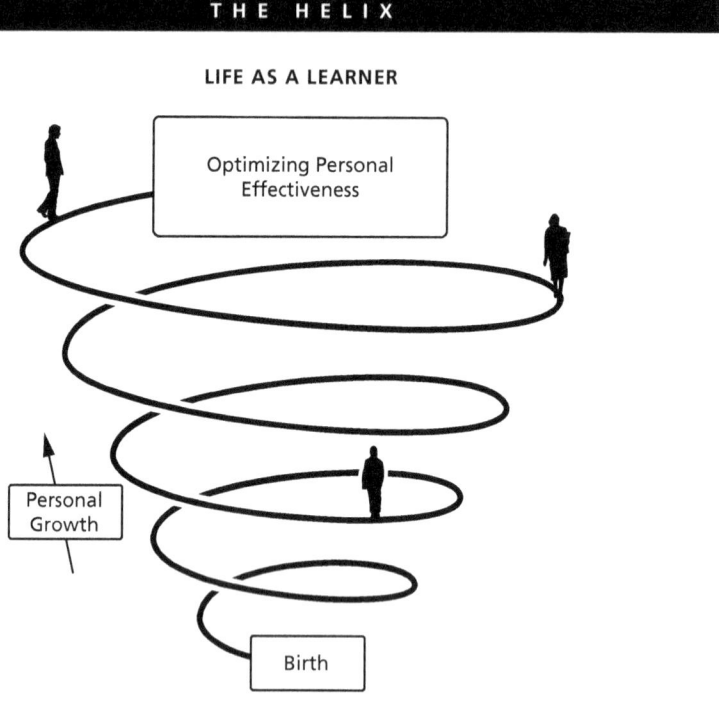

Over the years I have achieved varying results from engaging in the practices I believed would get me what I wanted. Sometimes I got the outcome I was looking for, but most often I did not. When I did not get what I expected, I blamed others and acted as if I was a victim of the world. Of course, nothing was ever wrong with me, and everything was wrong with the people, processes, organizations, technology, etc. that were challenging me.

Like the Traveler, I have lived more than half my life escaping from a past that consisted of circumstances I did not want to revisit and a family environment that revealed conflict between stated values and values in action. I didn't know what I wanted to do with my life, but I knew I did not want to be poor again. I did not want to be the victim.

I knew I liked nice things, and I wanted to be able to have all of the expensive toys I saw on TV. This is the simplicity of youth. What I would have to do to make this happen remained a mystery.

Eventually I realized that education was critical. So in good "Kevin fashion," I spent my first semester of college unconsciously striving for academic probation, and I spent the second semester consciously striving to get off of academic probation so I could continue the party. I barely made it, but my parents had had it. My dad and stepmother were paying, and I was playing. I don't think I went to class more than 30 times the whole first year of college and ended the year with a "C" average. My convenient excuse was that my parents owed it to me and that I would have done better if they had spent the money to send me to the college I wanted to attend (I actually had the grades to get in), rather than providing me with only two options from which to choose. I was the victim, and they were the oppressors. I just didn't get it. I transferred to a local college in Port Arthur and paid my own way from that point on. Nevertheless, after attending about two years of college, I barely had a "C" average and had probably dropped more classes than I had taken. The first year was on my parents; the rest was on me.

So my premise was that I'd need an education if I was to permanently rise above my circumstances. My practice was that I did not work very hard at getting an education. In fact, I was hard at work making my life more difficult by getting my girlfriend pregnant and increasing my level of responsibility. Next stop: the United States Air Force.

I joined the Air Force in 1984 and went through basic training and technical school. I ended up where I wanted to be: Denver, Colorado. The Air Force was the best thing that happened to me. I got to leverage my ability to endure no matter what. This was a skill that had been honed in my childhood and would serve me well later in life. I got excellent training and felt as though I was a part of something for the first time in my life. Nonetheless, I still knew better than anyone else and could not see the forest for the trees.

I went to several schools at night in an attempt to finish my degree. Again, I had attendance issues and often waited until the last minute to do my work. I also had part-time jobs that supported my overspending and inability to accept that I was still poor even though I had a job and benefits. I have never forgotten what it was like to be in survival mode for years on end.

By the time I reenlisted in the Air Force, I had two children from my first marriage and was into my second. I still had not taken ownership of my contributions to the failure of the first relationship or the problems I was having in the current one. Two more kids and seven years later, I was divorced again. However, along the way I finished my undergraduate degree and earned an MBA. I finished my MBA one day before separating from the Air Force. I achieved an "A" average in the courses I took to complete my undergraduate degree, and my average in my MBA was also an "A." Go figure.

So what happened? First, I was committed to my children, and I knew I would never be able to give them the life my father and stepmother had given me if I did not have an education. At least that is what I said. The reality was that it was about me. I wanted the house on the hill with the exotic sports car. I wanted everything I saw on the covers of magazines in the local grocery stores. Having that, I knew I would be happy. The ignorance factor struck again. Second, I was so unhappy that I finally channeled my frustration and energy into a positive direction. Of course I wish I had thought of that sooner. Third, I made friends in school (work by day and school by night). We sustained each other and, even though we didn't realize it, coached each other.

It was not until I was going through my second divorce and found myself on the path of entering yet another relationship that it moved into my consciousness. I realized that I had a pattern of behavior that reflected unconscious self-destruction.

One night, around ten, I was driving at an excessive speed while returning from teaching a class as an adjunct professor. I was driving a green sports car when a red turbo-charged version of the same car came up behind me out of nowhere. It went around me, got into my lane, and slowed down abruptly. I had to brake to keep from running into the back of the car.

I'd had a long day at work with another four hours tacked on teaching a class. And while I was going through my second divorce I was not in the best frame of mind. I changed lanes and floored it to pass the car and put some distance between us. Quite honestly, I really thought the person might be a drunk driver and I wanted to get as far away as possible. The next thing I knew, the car was on my rear end, so I slowed down so that the driver could drive around. Well, the car did go around, but it also cut in front of me and slowed down again. The rate of speed at which this happened caused me to immediately attempt to switch lanes to avoid hitting the car. I lost control of my car. I was traveling down the highway with my car spinning out of control. At that moment I knew I was going to die, and given my life circumstances at the time, it seemed the least painful outcome. I accepted my fate.

The first image that flashed into my mind was of my four children whom I would never again see. My next thought was whether I would suffer or if my death would be quick. Suddenly my car ran into the concrete embankment. First, the rear corner of the car, then the front corner, then the rear, then the front until the car finally came to a halt. I was alive and unharmed. The red car just kept going. No one stopped to help me. I was actually able to drive the car off the highway on three flat tires and ended up in the parking lot at a nearby school, where a security guard checked me out and gave me a ride home. What did I learn? Before I could learn anything, I had to process the experience. But I had to process the experience in the context of my entire existence and not just as an isolated event. I had questions. The most pressing question was, why did I engage in the behavior in the first place? Then, how did I get to the state of being I had reached? Why did I live? Who would I be if I had been severely injured?

I call these types of events "external compelling events."

They cause us to question our status quo. You would think that an experience like this would change a person for life. Unfortunately for me, it did not. It only got my attention until the crisis was over and I was able to rationalize it in the context of my normal behavior. I even went so far as to make it a point of conversation at parties. I was right back to being complacent about my behavior. No learning here. I was unconscious about the fact that I was lucky enough to get a second chance. I later realized that it was more like my 50th chance, and I still had many more mistakes to make before I finally decided to learn how to "attempt to" live consciously. I use "attempt" because, for me, it is a never-ending challenge. It is a journey.

My personal transformation point, relative to dealing with unconscious behavior, started when I was exposed to systems thinking concepts while working for a former employer. I was in that position for eight months and was immersed in the concepts through training, coaching, and some application. My friend Scott spent countless hours educating me on the tools, and I mapped the use of simulation tools to the human elements of change. However, I did not internalize what I had learned until after I returned to consulting. Slow learner. It was as though the train had left the station, but there were many miles before it would reach its destination. I had the information but I did not know how to apply it to myself. When I looked in the mirror, I was not able to see my true reflection.

It was not until I started Transformation Point and was writing the first version of our curriculum that I really internalized the concept of consciousness. I have spent the subsequent years experimenting on myself with small successes at first and then more significant levels of success once I increased my level of Alignment, a concept we'll discuss in the next chapter. The struggle to remain self-aware is like navigating multiple continuums that simultaneously span the gap between consciousness and unconsciousness. At any given point in time I am somewhere along the many continuums of focusing on other or self, being a team player or individualist, being present or distracted, in reflection or on the defensive, etc.

New Practices 1

The practices that I have internalized and use to maintain a higher degree of consciousness have evolved over time. The fundamental elements are as follows:

1. Pick a behavior to focus on that is getting in the way of your life satisfaction and overall success.
2. Determine who is impacted most by the behavior.
3. Determine what triggers the behavior. Remember you choose the behavior. No one is choosing your behavior for you.
4. List how the behavior aligns or misaligns with your goals.
5. List the impact to you if the behavior is not changed.
6. Get a coach, therapist, counselor to help identify the root dynamics of the behavior if you are not able to do so yourself (surface your thinking).
7. List the rules, biases, etc. that lead you to engage in the behavior. A good primer is "A person engages in _____ behavior because they..."

8. Outline the thought process that results in your selecting the behavior.
9. Outline the thought process that would lead your selecting a different behavior.
10. Develop a thought process for modifying your response to trigger events.
11. Explore alternative ways of thinking and acting.
12. Practice. Practice. Practice.
13. Ask for feedback from the people most impacted by the behavior.
14. Surround yourself with people who will challenge you and your behavior in a constructive fashion. In other words, they won't let you get away with it.
15. Get comfortable being challenged and having your perspective questioned. It is constant practice that increases my level of comfort with being challenged.
16. Adopt a learning mindset. Rather than engaging in challenging conversations to win, try engaging to learn.
17. Stop trying to be the smartest person in the room. Start being the person eliciting different perspectives and constructive conversations. I often say, "I am an absolute genius when I am in the room alone."

My ability to partner with others and increase the level of connection with my friends, family, clients, and business associates have all increased as a result of increased consciousness. But remember, it is a journey. I believe it is a destination that is never reached and a practice that is never perfected. The reason why I believe this is because the more successful I am at being conscious, the more complacent I become about the practice of being conscious. It is a constant struggle to anticipate complacency before it sets in. The list of action steps I have outlined above has helped me spend more time on the positive end of the consciousness continuum than the unconscious end. But beware! Being conscious without being personally aligned can lead to internal conflict and will negatively impact your ability to be your most effective self. More about that in the next chapter.

The Short of it...
   Understand your needs and then surface and confront your thinking in order to begin the journey to becoming your most effective self.

Reflections

Complete the following threads

1. When I am provided feedback that I don't agree with, my initial reaction is to_____. I react this way because…
2. I have very strong feelings about _____, and personally and professionally those feelings impact my ability to…
3. In the past, I believed _____ and later came to believe _____. What influenced me to change my perspective was…

4. When I am faced with changing my perspective I…
5. The people that I listen to the most who are able to get me to question my thinking are _____. They are effective because they…

"Align your purpose, goals, thinking, practices, passion, and find your authentic self."

[T H I N K !]

CHAPTER THREE

For quite some time, the Traveler reflected on his encounter with the Teacher of Consciousness. Once, while camping under the stars during a completely cloudless evening, he set a goal of sharing his mirror with willing others who may be interested in searching for their truth. He wondered whether this goal was realistic given the biases inherent in each person's perceptions of others and of themselves. He questioned if any person could be relied upon to accurately critique the reflections of themselves or others. How is it, he pondered, that a person could provide feedback without judgment or attribution? How could they become conscious of what they were unable see within themselves? He dozed off waiting for the stars to answer.

As he continued his journey, the Traveler realized that the City of Alignment was some distance from the City of Consciousness. Occasionally he stumbled upon villages seemingly made up of people who had discontinued their journeys. While he found them all to be wonderful hosts, he could not avoid becoming a little disappointed with their complacency. As he talked to several of the inhabitants of these villages, he noticed that they too spoke of 'the mirror Teacher.' He thought the reference to the Teacher of Consciousness was a bit unusual, and he felt disheartened that they had not been impacted as he had by the Teacher's questions. The Traveler assumed that they had perfected accepting themselves and one another as-is, but their personal growth seemed to have stopped there. In each village he visited, he noticed this same phenomenon. There seemed to be little growth among the people of these villages. They appeared to be comfortable and not striving to become their most effective selves. They did not complain about their conditions because they were content with their existence. The Traveler knew that this was not for him but did not realize that he was judging the villagers for choosing a destiny different from his own. However, he did begin to understand that he expected others to be as driven as he was. The Traveler still had much to learn about his biases and expectations of others. His perspective was that their lives would be better if they were more like him. He had much to learn about the lens through which he viewed the world.

He was relieved to finally see the City of Alignment in an approaching valley. Passing time, he reflected on the opportunities he found to practice what he had learned from the Teacher of Consciousness, but he found it difficult to be consistent in applying the teachings. Now he decided the time had come to align the teachings and his practices once and for all. He hoped to get the answers he was looking for from the Teacher of Alignment. He knew the answers he sought were inside of him. He just needed a guide to help him discover them. He hoped that this opportunity would provide him with the guidance he needed.

As he made his way down into the valley, the Traveler noticed that he was becoming apprehensive about entering the city. It was almost as if each step down the hillside presented a deeper sense of reservation. He recalled the conversation he had with the Teacher of Consciousness and the pain that came with the lessons learned from that experience. He wondered if this, too, would be painful. Was he ready for the challenges he would face? Could he handle another intense dive into self? Was this city the reason so many people became content living somewhere in the middle between Consciousness and Alignment?

By the time he reached the entrance to the city, he doubted himself severely, and he thought several times of turning back and altogether avoiding the city. But his body never stopped moving ahead, so before he could react to his fears he had entered the city and was greeted at the gates. He found the people were very friendly and seemed to glow with warmth and excitement. He asked a passerby where he could find Lorelei, the Teacher of Alignment, and was directed up a steep set of stairs to the Cascading Fountains.

As he approached the fountains he saw a figure kneeling before them. He waited in silence until the woman acknowledged his presence. She introduced herself as the Teacher of Alignment. He noticed that she did not use her first name. He said nothing of it, although it seemed peculiar. He could not help staring into her eyes because they sparkled and reflected an inner peace that he wished to discover for himself.

She began. "My brother informed me of your coming. I thought that you'd be here sooner. May I ask you why your journey took so long?"

He said that his journey had taken him many places that he had not anticipated visiting. He shared that he had discovered the journey from Consciousness to Alignment was a difficult one. He explained that he struggled with making the transformation from feeling to doing and that he still did not understand the source of his emotional reactions towards others. The Traveler went on to explain that often his thinking and his emotions were in conflict.

He told of his reluctance to enter the city, how he had considered turning back. Although he benefited from her brother's teachings, he had found the experience painful. "It took me a substantial amount of time to increase my consciousness. I am still struggling with maintaining it."

Eventually, the Traveler told her of his experiences along the way, of the small villages he visited, that in each village he learned something new about himself that caused him to question his very being. He revealed his tendency to judge others, especially if their choices did not align with his. The Traveler went on to reveal that challenging himself constantly had exhausted him, and he wondered if anyone could truly achieve and maintain a constant state of self-analysis. He guessed that many travelers would not have the patience to endure this.

Nearly identical to her brother, she began by asking him a pointed question. "What is most important for you to know and accept about yourself?"

He responded with a blank look before a simple "I do not know." A few seconds later he asked, "Do you mean that I should only be focusing on what is important to understand and accept about myself? How am I to know what is most important?"

She questioned him further. "What are your goals? What are you seeking? What must you accept about yourself in order for you to effectively pursue what you seek? What behaviors, beliefs, biases and fears prevent you from accomplishing your goals? What do you need to do to get out of your own way?"

The Traveler became frustrated with her almost immediately. "Slow down. I can't keep up with all of your questions. This feels like an interrogation!"

The Teacher continued, asking, "What is it that you have been thinking about over the last portion of your journey? Has it not occurred to you that my brother, the Teacher of Consciousness, had a reason for asking you to identify your destiny? Has it not occurred to you that my brother asked you about truth for a reason? You call yourself a Traveler, but I think wanderer would be more appropriate. Answer this: what is your purpose?"

The Traveler became furious and felt that he had been

insulted and judged. He now knew what this must feel like for others. His emotions were getting the better of him. With a shaky voice he answered, "My purpose is to contribute to the lives of others and to help other travelers as they travel on their journey without burdening them with my biases. And my practice, Teacher, is to learn what I can from you regardless of how painful the message may be."

"And what must you do in order to do this?"

He could not believe that she still asked questions of him. His emotions had to be obvious by this point. Nonetheless, he answered, "I must ensure that all my thinking and actions are aligned to accomplish this end. I must discover the values, beliefs, biases, behaviors and fears that could get in my way, and work on myself to ensure that my practices align with reaching my destiny."

"I see that the teachings my brother shared with you have not been wasted." He felt relieved that it was just a comment, but he was annoyed by her implication. She smiled at him and embraced him. She whispered into his ear, "Sometimes we need to be challenged a bit in order for us to see what may be obvious to others. It is not our practice to tell you what you should do, but it is our practice to challenge you and be an assistant to you as you grow into being your most effective self. When you took so long to get here, we grew concerned about you. We thought you were lost because it took you so long to arrive—especially after you seemed to embrace my brother's questions so eagerly."

Immediately his frustrations were relieved. The Traveler explained that he had many new experiences and found that with each new challenge he faced, he was predisposed to revert to his old thinking and practices. He told her that he found it difficult to focus on others more than he focused on himself and that he often found himself conflicted, caught between the person he claimed to be and the person he actually was. He shared that he wanted to be a catalyst for helping others challenge their thinking, to seek what was possible. "I did not realize that my journey would be so difficult. I always thought that I would get to a point where I could just relax and not have to think as much anymore. I have only come to discover that the requirement to think only increases. I don't seem to ever be able to let my guard down. My emotions seem to drive my thinking and my behavior."

"Tell me, Traveler. Have you ever learned to ride a bicycle?"

"In many of the cities I have visited, bicycles serve as the primary mode of transportation. I once lived with a family that owned one. It was a very valuable possession." He went on to tell her how one of their children had taught him how to ride the bicycle.

"And tell me. What was it like to ride it for the first time?"

"Frightening and exhilarating. I remember that there were so many things to pay attention to. I had to peddle, steer and balance all at the same time."

"And what was it like to ride after you had ridden the bicycle several times?"

"It was much less difficult. The more experience I had, the more comfortable I became and the less I had to think about the mechanics of riding. The emotional anxiety I felt was there in my stomach and I was constantly aware of it, but it was not as intense after I learned how to ride."

She asked, "How do you see learning to ride the bicycle in comparison to learning the concepts you have received from us?"

The Traveler reflected on the question for a few minutes before responding. "I think I get what you are asking. The more I practice these new learnings, the more comfortable I will become."

"Now tell me what you have learned from our conversation?"

The Traveler told her that he had learned that in order to reach alignment he needed to have a focus, or goal, and that his emotions, thinking, and resulting behavior needed to be aligned with these. He went on to explain that he needed to look within himself to identify what was missing or what was in the way and then determine what he needed to change in order to reach increasing levels of alignment. He told her that he could not help but question whether alignment was possible at all times.

"And why would it not be possible at all times?"

To this he responded, "I guess even if it were not possible I should be striving for it at all times. My challenge is to know myself and what drives my behavior and responses to situations. When I observe or engage with others, I feel emotions inside that I find myself reacting to. I feel an urge, a need to react a certain way, and I often don't understand the source of these emotions. At times I feel powerless to control my reactions in situations."

The Teacher listened attentively as the Traveler named his challenges with achieving alignment. She asked, "What do you know of authenticity?" The Traveler was once again caught off guard by her question. "Authenticity to me is being and modeling who we believe ourselves to be. It involves being true to ourselves and being honest with ourselves and others."

"And how do these emotions you speak of relate to authenticity?"

"I am not sure what you are getting at, but I think that they may be connected, in that my emotions are a result of my authentic feelings."

"What are your feelings a reflection of?"

To this the Traveler responded, "My feelings are a reflection of rules. When my rules are satisfied, I have little emotional reaction. But when my rules are not satisfied, I feel emotion and often react based on those feelings."

The Teacher then asked, "What are the sources of these rules?"

The Traveler was stumped but he knew his answer was important. The Teacher could see him in deep thought as he considered his answer. After several moments, the Traveler said, "My rules are the result of my learning, experience, and my natural tendencies. If my experience tells me that a rule works in producing the results I am looking for, then I tend never to question the rule. I guess you could say it becomes my bias. In fact, when I look at my natural or innate tendencies, I find that I tend to think that if I prefer to approach things a certain way then others should also approach things that way. I have a difficult time understanding why others do things as they do, especially when it is different from my way."

The Teacher asked, "Do you have a choice in how you respond to your feelings?"

The Traveler began to feel that the pieces were starting to come together. He answered, "I definitely have a choice, especially if my biases, rules and personal needs/preferences are clear and in my consciousness." He nodded, growing more confident as he spoke. "I think I am getting it now. I not only have to be conscious of the rules and biases that influence my thinking and behavior, I also should be conscious of my needs and emotions. In the larger scheme, my needs drive my emotions, my emotions drive my actions, and my actions either align with my ability to achieve authenticity, or they don't. This would mean that I have to make conscious choices about how I will respond to the emotions associated with my needs not being met. Further, I will need to develop the ability to name when my needs are not being met and to choose an appropriate response—a response that aligns with being authentic but also respectful of other's needs."

The Teacher smiled and told the Traveler that he was truly beginning to understand the essence of her thinking. She asked him to consider the possibility that reaching a destination may not be as important as striving to be the best and most complete person he could as he continued his journey. The Teacher also explained that recognizing and sharing his challenges with others often reduces the anxiety associated with achieving and maintaining personal alignment.

The Traveler replied, "I can already feel my anxiety diminishing and my energy increasing."

The Teacher could not resist the temptation to drill further into his comment on his energy. "What role does your energy play in your ability to sustain yourself?"

The Traveler smiled and realized that he had set himself

up for her question. "My energy is how I sustain myself. I am finding that I must maintain a high level of energy in order to have tolerance and to engage in the practices I am developing. I recognize I only have so much capacity to maintain consciousness and alignment. In order to increase my resiliency, I will need to be deliberate in my efforts to tap into that which brings me energy and to minimize the amount of time I am engaged with that which drains my energy. It is in this centered state that I can find peace and reenergize." At that moment a new thought occurred to him, and he asked the Teacher a very thoughtful question. "As I grow and learn more and become a better person, how will the people in my life know that I have changed?"

She again smiled at him and told him he would find his answer with her sister in the City of Reinvention. He smiled and said, "I should have known. Does your sister have a name?"

"Sarah."

They wished each other farewell before he picked up his baggage and chose his path toward the City of Reinvention. He noticed this time that the bag he had brought with him from the City of Consciousness felt quite a bit lighter than when he had arrived.

DISCUSSION

The research of James Kouzes and Barry Posner, *Credibility* (1993) and *The Leadership Challenge* (1995), Peter Senge, *The Fifth Discipline* (1990), Joseph Badaracco, Jr., *Defining*

Moments (1997), Chris Argyris and Donald Schön, *Theory in Practice* (1974), Ed Oakley and Doug Krug, *Enlightened Leadership* (1991), and Nathaniel Branden, *The Psychology of Self-Esteem* (1969) and *The Six Pillars of Self-Esteem* (1994) discuss different aspects of alignment and the associated impact on our professional and personal lives. Modeling behavior that is consistent with what we preach is one aspect of alignment. Even more exciting, alignment that connects us with our passion creates the path for us to operate at the level of our potential.

    I spent the vast majority of my career shaping myself into a money-making machine. If you offered 25-30% more than what I was making currently, then you had my ear. Tell me I wasn't qualified for the next level position, and I went into the market and proved you wrong. In the ten years following my separation from the Air Force I went from Business Analyst to Vice President. I left no dollars on the table in the process. I could sell myself into anything I decided I wanted to do and then do it. Most of the time, in addition to pursuing my career, I was also teaching as an adjunct professor and enrolled in a doctoral program. The distance between me and my past circumstances was increasing, but I would not let myself get comfortable, for the constant fear of returning to where I started was always in my mind. I was living the dream on the outside, but the inside was an entirely different story.

    I had a high level of consciousness of my external practices. In other words I knew which behaviors would get the results I was looking for professionally. I modeled any practice that led to success. I knew what to do to get what I wanted. This became a competency. But I had not yet done the hard work of tackling the internal dynamics that were driving my behavior. I had not tackled my thinking. I created a mask for every occasion and enacted the practices that breathed life into the character. There was little alignment between what I was doing and what I was feeling. I was as a chameleon. I was not congruent.

On the inside I was bored within six months of every job I ever had–I had no passion for what I was doing, But I knew I wanted to work for myself someday. I had two simple rules. First, I didn't want to be told what to do. Second, I wanted to be the master of my own destiny... on my timeline. Inside I was unhappy, unfulfilled, and afraid of failing. You could probably make an argument that everyone saw it but me, but it didn't seem that way to me, and it certainly didn't stand in the way of me getting what I wanted almost all of the time. Enter Lisa.

I met Lisa while attending the first year of a doctoral program. I was studying Human Communications Studies, and she was in graduate school studying International Management. By some scheduling miracle we ended up in the same Quality Management class and in the same study group. Her eyes sparkled.

Lisa challenged me from our first conversation. I was doing my best impersonation of a person who had it all together, and she was demonstrating her proficiency in calling "bull." What a combination. I didn't ask her out until the class was nearly over, but our relationship blossomed and, despite her intelligence, she decided to marry me, deal with my ex-wives, my kids, and me to boot. She deserves a very special reward.

The first three years were hell. I was busy being right all

of the time, and she was busy setting me straight. Lisa has been the most patient person I have ever known. She would not back down until I finally faced myself. I was so conflicted and blind that the person I am now would probably have taken that old me out into an alley and kicked my butt a few times. Lisa would not let me get away with anything, but she was not working with fertile ground. I was hardened. Thankfully, she persevered. About eighteen months into our marriage, we got custody of my two older daughters from my first marriage. I was working for one of the "Big 6" consulting firms at the time and was traveling a significant amount of the time. Lisa was now a full-time single parent to two kids that were not her own (you wouldn't know it from how she treated them) and half-time parent to my other two kids from my second marriage. Of course, I was constantly rationalizing that I needed to stay with the firm.

One night, Lisa, my good friend Dennis, his significant other Joscelyn and I were having a conversation. At that time, the topic of all conversations was how great our jobs were and the projects we were working on at the firm. We were gods. Lisa and Joscelyn told us that we could not see ourselves and that we were like androids. Of course I argued that I was not and that they did not know what they were talking about.

Six months later I changed jobs and took a local job for eight months. I then took another consulting job for a year during which I spent six months on the road. Is anything wrong with this picture? My stated goal was to be the best father I could, but my behavior was not aligned. I had a story for everything and could rationalize anything I decided to do. I had a history of this, yet Lisa would not back down.

One night I was at a local restaurant waiting for a friend to arrive. He was late, and I was people-watching and listening to the conversations. It happened that a group of consultants from the "Big 6" firm I had worked for were having a gathering there. As I listened to their conversations I was struck: I finally got what Lisa and Joscelyn had described. I won't go into the details of their discussions about their own genius, but I saw a vision of me that I could not rationalize away. For the first time in years, I was embarrassed to be me. The ground was now fertile, and Lisa started planting anything she thought would grow. No weeds allowed. But it would be another three years before that garden would yield a thing.

The Garden Begins to Yield

Mom died. I sat in the house on the hill and played chess with my son, Bryce. I couldn't even cry about it.

My son asked, "Why haven't you cried about Bonnie dying?"

I told him, "It's a long story, man. I've been hurt by her so many times that I just sort of cut off my feelings for her."

"Then it's like playing chess, Dad. She made moves she couldn't take back."

My son became the teacher, and my tears began to flow. A few days later I spoke at her funeral and it was difficult to hold back the tears. For the first time in many years I was able to focus on the good in her and opened myself up to really feel for the first time in years. She did the best she could, and she suffered more than any person should have to. She endured drug addiction, abuse by boyfriends and my stepfathers, mental institutions, sterilization, and shock treatments.

She had finally found peace, and in her death I found the beginning of my own inner peace.

Lisa now saw a side of me she had never seen. I was vulnerable and open. My children saw me in a different light as well. My work was just beginning. Family became a much greater focus, although I continued to take it for granted. My relationships with my children were now much more important to me, and I could see how much they needed me and could feel how much I needed them. This still was not enough.

Lisa's hard work and persistence was paying off. I think she placed the right bet.

The journey was long, and it continues today. Like the Traveler, I now had a purpose and a focus. Life was no longer just about me; it was also about them. I found myself reaching back to the practices of consciousness to help me become aligned. But even with such a great awakening, I realized that focus and purpose alone were not enough.

It was not until I founded Transformation Point and completed the initial design of our curriculum that I discovered I was passionate about helping people, and ultimately organizations, face their challenges. My emphasis was on helping people to transform their lives personally and professionally. With the exception of my family, nothing has been more inspiring to me. I found my purpose and my passion. This discovery was yet another step in striving to be aligned in all that I do.

As you can see, alignment is no easy task, and it is inextricably linked to consciousness. Without consciousness alignment is not possible. We have to be conscious of our misalignment before we can address it. What I have learned is that I had to be open, virtually turned inside out, before I got it. Now, after many hours of reflection, I see the simplicity of my problem. I was not ready or willing to transform; therefore, I was not capable of transforming. Founding Transformation Point was the catalyst for my journey because it immersed me in concepts that helped me to understand my own misalignment. It helped me make the connection between learning, thinking systematically, and transformation.

New Practices 2

The practices that I have internalized and use to maintain a higher degree of alignment have also evolved over time.

The fundamental elements are as follows:

1. Identify your passion and your purpose.
2. If what you are doing is not aligned with your passion and purpose, identify the cause.
3. Prioritize what is most important to you, and align your choices with your priorities.
4. Define your desired self.
5. If you are not your desired self, identify what is in the way and why.
6. Determine what is missing in your everyday life personally and professionally.
7. Map out an incremental plan to fill the voids.
8. Spend a portion of every day reflecting on your interactions to identify gaps between what you intended to do and what you actually did, and between who you intended to be and who you actually were.

9. Create a plan to close the gaps between your daily goals and your actual behavior.
10. List the top five characteristics you want to be synonymous with hearing your name or seeing your face. That is your personal brand, and should be consistent with your goals, passion, beliefs, and values. Next, compare your desired brand with your words and actions. Finally, you must internalize thinking that is consistent with your desired brand in order to produce the results you are looking for. My quality of life and the quality of my relationships have improved as a result of becoming more personally aligned. My choices are aligned with my goals, and my behavior (on most days) aligns with my personal brand. This has resulted in a much higher level of life satisfaction. I am energized by who I am and what I do. I am inspired when I am able to inspire others.

The Short of it...

Align your purpose, goals, thinking, practices, passion, and find your authentic self.

Reflections

Complete the following threads.

1. I see inconsistencies in myself in the areas of...
2. Others have challenged me about inconsistencies in my...
3. For me, not being aligned results in...
4. In the last 30 days I have received the following feedback related to my alignment...
5. It is difficult for me to be aligned because...
6. I am able to model _____ behavior(s) but inside I am thinking and feeling...

"As we grow and learn, we will inevitably discover the need to reinvent ourselves and recover from that which we did not know or would not acknowledge about ourselves."

[**T H I N K !**]

CHAPTER FOUR

Departing the City of Alignment, the Traveler recognized the positive energy and diminished anxiety he felt after his encounter with Lorelei. He was so determined to practice processing his experiences that he concluded his existence was about his journey more than about arriving at any destination. He was beginning to believe that each stop along his journey was like an interim destination, a place to pause, reflect, and refocus before continuing on. While he was somewhat taken aback by this possibility, he also was encouraged by it. Each time he moved on he was better for the experience and more equipped to continue his journey. He was gaining new tools and new perspectives. This was the most exciting challenge he'd ever faced. With each stop along the way, the Traveler found himself ready to pick up new tools that would help him on the next leg of his journey. He began to focus more on the next stop and much less on the destination he had once set for himself, for he realized that each stop provided new truths and enlightenment. He now felt a sense of freedom and found peace in knowing that his perspective would change if he left himself open to experiencing his journey as a seeker of growth opportunities—an explorer of new thinking.

Armed with new knowledge and new perspectives, the Traveler again contemplated how people would know that he had changed. This was the focal point of his reflection for the remainder of his first day back on foot. As the day wore on and dusk approached, he happened upon a camp where other travelers had gathered for the evening.

"Would you all mind terribly if I joined you for the evening?"

Without question, they welcomed him into their camp. After his eyes adjusted fully to the firelight, the Traveler began to take notice of his companions. He recognized some of the other travelers in the camp. One woman had shared a path with him for a short while, although he remembered her voice more than her face. Her wisdom was quite impressive. Still others he had encountered more recently. He could not be sure if they recognized him.

Each member of the camp made a contribution to the evening's meal. Some supplied bread, and others supplied herbs, while others tossed in vegetables. Soon a handful of new arrivals added fresh fish to the meal that was caught in a nearby stream. As they worked together to prepare their meal, they shared tales of their travels. The Traveler was encouraged when he noticed that several of his hosts told of their failures, treating them no differently than their success stories. The exchange of stories became an exchange of ideas and the thinking behind those ideas. Most experiences had elements common to many, and the Traveler was glad to have a chance to chime in from time to time with tales from his own journey.

While chewing bread, one gentleman spoke up about having met the Traveler before. The Traveler did not recognize his acquaintance until the man spoke of spending several days traveling a very rocky trail together. According to his story, he and the Traveler learned a great deal about each other during their parallel journey and discovered that they disagreed often.

"Of course. I remember you now. We could not agree about giving."

The Traveler was an only child and traveled alone, so he was not accustomed to sharing. His former companion believed that one should share his possessions freely without expecting another to give in return. He believed that it is natural for people to give—that one should give from the heart.

"It is a truly human act, one of desire instead of obligation." This was his rule and he believed in it as strongly as if it were a law or universal truth.

"I remember," began the Traveler, "that I did not agree with this belief."

"Yes, my friend. You are correct. If you remember as well, you went to great lengths to account for each of our contributions. If I contributed a potato to our stew, you felt it your duty to add a carrot or some other item."

"Yes, and we argued constantly because you wanted to rob me of the opportunity to be an equal giver. That became a very frustrating ordeal for me."

"I'm sure it was a frustrating time for you, but please know that I only wanted you to know that you did not have to contribute equal amounts to be considered my equal. A person's value cannot be measured solely by their possessions or contributions. There is something much deeper that reflects one's value. However, I again am sorry to have created such frustration for you then."

To this the Traveler replied, "I have learned much about myself and my rules since that time. I have changed much about myself since our time together."

During this interaction, the other members of the camp remained quiet. Some seemed to reflect on the conditions of the evening, while others attended to their supplies or simply listened to the present conversation.

Having just finished a rather pleasant reunion with a former companion, the Traveler had no idea that another past traveling companion was also within the camp. While the Traveler contributed to the meal, he took notice of others' contributions and compared them to his own. He considered himself rather fortunate recently, so he ate sparingly so that those with less to offer would have more to eat.

This other fellow, though, noticed this, too.

After recognizing the feeling of someone's eyes fixed on

him, the Traveler decided to acknowledge the man. "I believe that we have traveled together before, have we not?"

"You are correct, and you have not changed," was his condescending response.

"That certainly is not so. In fact, I have learned much since we last met." He went on to share stories of how he spent significant time with different teachers and worked to change his thinking. This effort to prove himself was to no avail. His former companion simply would not accept that he had changed, no matter how much evidence the Traveler provided. Apparent to all, the Traveler became frustrated.

A couple of the men who had traveled with the Traveler commented on their own experiences with him. One responded, "I have also traveled with this man, and I do not know the person you describe. I only know him to be who he says he is."

To this the man replied, "He is a fraud," and abruptly walked away.

The conversation died and the men rose to turn in for the evening; it was apparent that they could do nothing to remedy the situation. The Traveler thanked the two men for their support; then he prepared his bed for the evening. In the back of his mind the volume rose on the question that had been nagging him. "How will people know I have changed?" He would not rest well that evening.

The next morning the Traveler woke before the others. He did not want any further confrontation and wanted to move on with his journey. He was anxious to get to the City of Reinvention to have help with this dilemma of having a "before" and "after" identity—of not being recognized for who he had become versus who he had been. As he walked on, he replayed the events of the prior evening. His mind attempted to rationalize much of his dissonance. "Why is it so important to me that people recognize that I have changed? Why should I care about convincing them? What should I do when people won't recognize my changes in light of all of the evidence that indicates otherwise? His attempts to make sense of it all failed. The Traveler's pace quickened as he made his way toward the City of Reinvention. While he was haunted by the questions his encounter had made even more pressing, he was also searching hard for the answers.

After less time than he expected, the Traveler arrived at the City of Reinvention. His preoccupied state of mind made the time and distance pass by with little notice. He barely recognized his fatigue and hunger, driven as he was to get answers to his questions.

Entering the city, he noticed several construction projects underway. In fact, everywhere he looked, he saw structures being destroyed, built or remodeled. He had never seen anything like it. He wondered what was driving all of this simultaneous development and decided to ask this of the Teacher as well. "Maybe that'll get our conversation going," he thought. As he made his way past one of the construction zones he asked one of the workers where he might find the Teacher of Reinvention. The woman told him that he would find her in her art studio, Identity, near the museum.

The Traveler had no trouble finding the studio, and it, too, had construction workers hanging from ropes and scaffolding and working on the façade of the building. As he entered the studio he found that renovations were being made inside as well. He wondered if the other buildings also were having work done on their interiors. The Traveler navigated his way around the various construction zones inside the studio and followed the signs directing him to a temporary showroom. There he found the Teacher of Reinvention positioning a sculpture atop one of the pedestals. He began to introduce himself but was interrupted.

"Are you the Traveler? I believe that my sister sent you here to see me."

"Yes. How did you know?"

"I have been expecting you, and I can tell by your expression you are eager to ask me many questions. My sister warned me that you had a pressing question for me. What is it?"

The Traveler had hardly caught his breath. As he looked around the room his question seemed less important than his curiosity about the pieces in the room. "The question can wait. Tell me about your studio and the pieces you have here. It seems that there is a theme to each piece but I can't quite put my finger on what it is."

"What do you find so intriguing about these pieces?"

"They seem to change depending on how you look at them. I can't find words to describe them, because each view seems to contradict the other."

"Is the view a contradiction of the other, or is it complimentary?" asked the Teacher.

"I can't explain it."

"Yet you are attempting to. Why is this?"

The Traveler was struggling to answer when he realized her question was at the heart of his own. Without answering her question he asked, "Why are people unable to accept others who have changed?"

"Is that your question?" she asked.

Not prepared to commit to his answer, the Traveler hesitated before responding. "No," he said finally. "My question is, why do we paint others into boxes we won't let them out of no matter how much they change?"

Engaged in her visitor's question, the Teacher replied, "What is changing? Who is the painter? What benefit is gained from placing and keeping others in boxes? What can we own about allowing ourselves to fit neatly into a box in the first place? If we commit ourselves to continually learning, growing, and modeling our development and growth in our thinking through our actions, can we really be confined to one box?"

Fully aware that she was overwhelming her visitor, she continued, "Once we have demonstrated that our thinking and perspective have changed through our actions, what is the purpose of trying to convince others of our growth? Is there value in broadcasting to others the changes we make, so they understand that we recognize the need to change and are working to change? Is your goal to change the essence of who you are, or is it to change who you are being? Exactly how would you go about changing your essence? There is no need to answer these questions this moment. In fact, one could spend a lifetime pondering the answers to these questions and find that his answers change and evolve over time. However, the value is in taking the time to think about the relevance of both the questions and the answers to one's journey."

Seeming not to take a breath she continued, "Let me take

you upstairs and show you where you will be staying tonight. After you have rested for a while, we can continue our conversation over dinner." He willingly followed her to his quarters.

He was pleased to have a bedroom and a bathroom, more comfortable accommodations than his camping offered. She left him to return to her studio.

He bathed and took a long nap. When he awoke it was early evening. He dressed and returned to the studio where he found the Teacher unpacking a sculpture. "Are you ready for dinner?" she asked.

"Whenever you complete what you are doing. Might I be of any assistance to you?"

"I can finish this tomorrow," she responded. "I have prepared a meal for us in my apartment next door. Shall we?"

The Traveler followed her as she made her way through the studio and to a door that connected to her apartment. "That's convenient," said the Traveler.

"It is. See, I am so passionate about my work I find that being near my creations energizes me. It is an incredible feeling to create works that engage people and cause them to challenge their perspectives, as you did when you looked at the pieces for the first time. This is both my passion and my purpose. My brother, the Teacher of Consciousness, gave you a mirror before you parted. Do you have it with you?"

"Yes." He removed the mirror from his pocket. Sarah walked him over to one of the pieces in her apartment and instructed him to stand before it and move the mirror slowly around the piece so that he could see it from multiple perspectives at once. The Traveler did as she instructed.

"What do you see?" she asked.

"I see the complete piece from multiple views," replied the Traveler.

"What meaning does this have to your question of how others view you and the changes you have made?"

He thought for a while. "People often only see us from a few vantage points at a time and define us based upon that view. I guess it would be difficult to get a full view of any person unless you were able to see him in all aspects of life, especially the areas that have meaning for him. So depending on what is important to the viewer, they may not recognize changes in areas that they don't see or that are not meaningful to them. More importantly, they cannot see the changes you have made on the inside. They can't see the changes in your thinking. However, it would also seem that the viewer has to be willing to see the changes before them. They have to be open to interpreting your intent differently than they did before and setting their judgments aside. We have no control over this. We can only be authentic and congruent."

"Let's sit down and eat," said the Teacher as she took him by the arm and led him to the dinner table.

Once they were seated, the Traveler wondered what the Teacher thought of his answer. He waited for her to volunteer any comments. She did not. The Traveler then asked, "I answered your question but would like to know your thoughts about my answer."

"What about your answer has meaning for you?" she asked. "Did you get to the heart of the matter? Has your answer relieved you of the anxiety you had when you asked your question?"

To the Traveler's amazement he realized that he truly had

found within himself the answer to his question. "I am the painter. I decide who needs to recognize my changes. I decide the effort I want to expend convincing others. I must prepare my environment to accept my changes. My actions have more meaning than my words. If I continue to grow and learn, I will outgrow any box others may perceive me into. I am accountable!" he shouted with a smile on his face.

"Easier said than done," was her reply. "You will find this out when you visit my father in the City of Accountability."

The smile fell from the Traveler's face but soon returned. He was growing accustomed to having to continually work on improving himself and knew his meeting with the Teachers' father would be an opportunity for him to improve even more. He and the Teacher talked about many other things as they finished their meal.

Later, after helping the Teacher clean up, he returned to his room and thought of what was in store for him in the City of Accountability. It did not take long for him to fall asleep.

The next morning, he had breakfast with the Teacher before he departed.

"Thank you for your assistance. I hope that I am figuring out more of what it takes for me to gain truth. This was a short visit, but it has been so helpful. Maybe more than you know."

"I bid you farewell, and I wish you safe travel."

He picked up his bag and found his path while wondering what was in store for him on this next phase of his journey. As he walked he saw his shadow and noticed that he stood erect with no bend in his back. He did not know what had caused this. He quickly dismissed it from his thoughts as he began to think about the next stop on his journey.

Discussion

Of the books and articles I have read, Stephen Covey's *The Seven Habits of Highly Effective People* (1989) best captured the essence of reinvention in his discussion of "The Emotional Bank Account." (Covey, 1989, p.188-203) This chapter also comes from the battlefield of life through making mistakes and paying for them, from recognizing the damage one does to others that can only be repaired through atonement, and from committing to focus on others in pursuit of self.

Reinvention is reconstruction from the inside out. It is about finding the truth in feedback. It starts with assessing how you are perceived and how those perceptions impact your ability to be effective, and then mapping out a strategy to modify your thinking and resulting behavior to align with the authentic personal brand you desire. Imagine a time when you were in a meeting or at a dinner party and you said or did something that created a negative impression. Sometimes we don't get to recover from these types of errors, and that first impression influences how people interact with us and interpret our behavior and words for as long as we know them. More importantly, mistakes from our past may limit our opportunities. This could be considered creating a negative brand—being brand negative.

In other situations we may be on our best game. We create an impression that is positive. This, too, influences how others interact with us and interpret our behavior and words. This could be considered creating a positive brand, or being brand positive.

Each of us currently has a personal brand. You might think of it as the five things that are synonymous with hearing your name or seeing your face. Of course it could be greater or fewer than five things, but they represent the way you are perceived by others. In every interaction we have, verbal or nonverbal, our brands are being communicated. More importantly, they may be helping us or hindering us. Consequently, if you don't know your current brand, you can't manage it. It manages you! This becomes a critical factor when you are leading change and/or attempting to engage employees.

One important aspect of reinvention is determining who are your blockers, enablers, and neutrals. Blockers are people with whom you are brand negative. They operate against you. Enablers are people with whom you are brand positive. They work on your behalf. Neutrals are those people who don't have an opinion one way or the other. They represent an opportunity for you when you are building your coalition of personal and professional supporters.

Another key aspect of reinvention is that your brand is in the room when you are not. For example, someone once told me that in some of their company meetings people could not take paper out of the room, because in those meetings they decided the futures of their key talent. In the discussions it was apparent who were the enablers, blockers and neutrals for the individuals being discussed. Do you have a personal brand strategy? Do you know who your enablers, blockers, and neutrals are? Do you have a strategy in place to sustain your relationships with your enablers, neutralize or enhance your relationships with your blockers, and convert neutrals to enablers? This is the essence of reinvention.

In the pursuit of our own goals we may impede the pursuits of others. While attempting to manage the impression we create, we may unintentionally or intentionally make someone else appear less impressive. This is the nature of competition and reflects a mindset of scarcity rather than abundance. In some cases this is a conscious pursuit, and in others it may be unconscious. Regardless of the intent, the outcome is the same. Harm is done to others in more ways than we may understand. The damage is not always external; sometimes it strikes at the core of another person's existence. Now imagine the impression that is made when you are not only being impressive yourself but also helping others promote themselves by supporting their efforts to impress. (This assumes that the impression they are trying to make is backed up by substance.) These are the types of people who inspire others and achieve uncommon results. This is an excellent brand element to have.

Once you know what you want your brand to be, you need to assess your desired brand against your actual brand to identify the gaps. Basically, you need to conduct a 360-degree assessment, or personal and professional brand audit, to see the level of alignment you currently have between your desired brand and your actual brand. This information should feed your personal action plan to bring the two into alignment. It may sound simple, but it's not.

Remember that you have blockers and neutrals that are not necessarily on your side. How will they know you have changed on the inside? Think of it this way: you are in a box, and you have to figure out how to get out of it. Again, not so simple! Especially, if you put yourself there through your own actions. There are forces at work trying to keep you in the box. And you are one of them! You must figure out what you need to do to get out of the box you're in and neutralize the forces focused on keeping you there. Time to start working out!

The Teacher of Reinvention asked the Traveler to look at a sculpture from multiple perspectives to gain a more holistic interpretation. People see us from different perspectives based on the context of the interactions they have with us. The hard work is in taking ownership of our contribution to their interpretation of our brands. I will elaborate on this more in the next chapter. Our responsibility to ourselves is to be conscious of our behavior and our brand, become aligned, and understand the reinvention we need to accomplish and with whom.

Like the Traveler using the mirror to gain a 360-degree perspective of the statue, we must look at issues with our personal brand from not only our perspective but from the perspectives of others. We must then be able to empower ourselves to take ownership of our contribution to any problem areas and then take action to resolve those issues. Changing another person's perception can be frustrating, if not impossible. Internalizing and modeling behavior that is consistent with your desired brand can still result in others' perceptions becoming distorted.

Distortion occurs when you have internalized new thinking and modeled behavior that is consistent with your desired brand, but others continue to engage with you as if you were modeling behaviors consistent with your old brand and thinking. For example, if your old brand was that you focused more on self than others, and your new brand is to focus more others than self, an individual observing your new other-oriented behavior may not recognize it. This could be because cognitively they have difficulty matching your new behavior with your old brand. They still see you in the self-oriented box and behave toward you in ways consistent with their perception. They may even misinterpret your actions in ways that allow them to still see you as they always have. You are in the box, and they are trying desperately to keep you there. In most cases, they are not conscious of what they are doing. They are just busy trying to be efficient and not pausing long enough to recognize the change in the dynamics at play.

Another individual, observing that the response you are getting to your other-oriented behavior is not appropriate, may have difficulty reconciling why you are being treated like you are self-oriented. They then may perceive the person you are interacting with as being inappropriate. This is positive distortion because it works in your favor. It creates a force that operates without you doing anything except internalizing new thinking and modeling behavior consistent with your desired brand. The force is like multi-level marketing. Focus on the people who accept your new brand, and they will influence others on your behalf. And what of the people who won't accept that you have changed? Let the forces handle them. Inevitably, they will interact with you inappropriately in the wrong setting with the wrong audience, and then they will likely have their own branding issue. Stay focused on what you need to own and keep making the changes you need to make to be brand consistent.

In my life, I certainly have had to reinvent myself every time I undertook a personal transformation as a result of learning, changing my thinking, and growing as person, parent, husband, son, friend, professional, etc. As I outlined in the story of my struggles with alignment, I was a chameleon. I could model whatever behaviors I needed to get what I wanted. This is not the type of branding I am referring to. I am referring to a sincere effort to model the behaviors consistent with fulfilling my personal mission statement.

What are the five universal bullet points you want everyone to agree on when conducting your memorial service? The real stuff!

The negative characteristics I have actively worked to overcome through the years are:
1. Selfish
2. Unconscious
3. Incongruent
4. Arrogant
5. Dogmatic

The brand I want to be synonymous with hearing my name or seeing my face includes (not in order of priority):
1. Committed to helping others
2. A great friend
3. A great coach
4. Making a difference
5. Impactful but also fun

I work toward modeling my desired brand in all of my interactions and to be constantly improving in each area of my personal brand. It is a focus. It is a journey. However, it is not perfection.

The process I have used over the past several years is to pick a few key focus areas for the year and work on them actively. This past year I spent the majority of my time working to focus on others more than on myself. The feedback I have received indicates that I have been successful in doing this. My personal revelation is that you have to be careful whom you commit to doing this with because some people take advantage of it. The upside is that you get to have some wonderful internal dialogue about your level of commitment to the goal and your motives. I believe I started down this path because of the greater good focus and found that it was very difficult to not think about self. Key learning: It is easier to focus on others when there is abundance and more difficult in times of scarcity.

One year I was focusing on being a better coach and friend to my family. I went to visit my paternal grandparents and my father and stepmother. My grandparents were bedridden and in the last stage of their lives. I went to say goodbye to my grandmother who had recently been released from intensive care. She seemed to have lost her will to live. I have made this type of trip before when my maternal grandmother was ill. Not pleasant.

In the course of this visit, I realized that at the rate we were going my father and I would likely only see each other about ninety times over the next thirty years. I would be doomed to pay yet another last visit to someone I loved.

My father is 71. I love him dearly, and we generally have great conversations. He is an amazing listener and his heartfelt attention makes me know that he feels my pain and understands my struggle. I would love to see him more than two to three times a year, and I will. We are committed to this, and I am accountable for keeping my end of the deal.

We both enjoy my visits and our conversations. In one conversation I told him that the past was in the past, and that I wanted us to focus on the present and the future. He paused and looked at me from across the table. Too much time wasted. My point was made.

It is amazing how making a statement to which you are committed can change the trajectory of a relationship. It was like playing chess, as my son said. I made a move I couldn't (wouldn't) take back.

On July 16, 2005 I thought my son was going to die. We were in Italy that summer, and he collapsed and had to be hospitalized there for over three weeks and several more weeks once we returned home. This presented the hardest time of my life. Not only was he hospitalized, but he also was in restraints, and I had to help the nurses and doctors keep him in them. It was hell.

Through the course of his recovery, I learned a lot about what I needed to do to become his friend. Our conversations have changed: I talk to him like a coach now instead of a parent. A major improvement! My brand as coach and friend are yielding results.

My youngest daughter, Blayre, has developmental disabilities. She suffers from microcephaly and cerebral palsy. Blayre is my best friend. She has taught me so many things about myself and about how to put someone else's needs before my own. Before you can understand this in context, I will have to tell you the story of my best friend Blayre.

Blayre is 25 and has to be cared for like a toddler. This is important to know because she is the size and stature of a 7 or 8 year-old and has many of the needs of an infant. She is about 4 feet tall and weighs about 80 pounds. She can't talk in words and she can't walk on her own without assistance. She can't feed herself with utensils. She basically has to be assisted with all activities. There are a lot of things Blayre can't do.

What can Blayre do? She can look at you in a way that makes you feel that you are the only person in the world. She can hug you and make all your stress and problems go away in a moment. She can teach you how to love unconditionally. Blayre teaches you how to manage yourself so that you can interact with her and give her what she needs. Blayre teaches you how to listen with all your senses. Most importantly, Blayre teaches authenticity.

Blayre can't fake it. If she is upset, you know it. If she doesn't want to be touched, you know it. If she is ready to eat, you really know it! Imagine working for someone who only wants what they want and has no capacity to accept no, not now, or wait. This is Blayre. You move at her pace not yours. Well, you can move at yours but you will have to hear the loudest most pitiful crying you have ever heard. You can get angry and frustrated. You can give up, or you can learn to manage yourself and modify your process.

What is a typical day like with my Blayre? Generally speaking, Blayre is calm and content. However, she can be difficult to deal with when she is annoyed, or things are not moving at her desired pace. You have to accept this, because you can't change it or control it. This means I have to expect her to be annoyed and be surprised by contentment. In other words, I have no control, but I have a lot of influence. My Influence comes from who I choose to be in our interactions. I choose to be positive and understanding. I talk to her constantly when she is yelling at me, which serves two purposes. It acknowledges her emotion and second, allows me to express what I think she is feeling constructively and take ownership of what I may not be doing. Remember, I am guessing because she can't tell me. I call this our relationship building time. I show understanding, and she shows more patience.

I typically put Blayre to bed consistently at the same time. This does not mean that I can expect her to go to sleep or wake up consistently at the same time. Blayre wears Pull-Ups. I double them to cut down on accidents. Otherwise the day starts with changing sheets, washing laundry, and a bath at 5 or 6AM. Next, I get up at 5 or 6AM to change Blayre and give her water.

Morning routine with Blayre: Prepare breakfast prior to getting Blayre up. Why? She expects everything to be prepared when she gets to the kitchen. Otherwise, that screeching sound I spoke of earlier occurs. Not the way you want to start your day. Then I get Blayre up on the toilet, brush teeth, do hair, bathe (if not the night before), dress, and off to the kitchen to eat.

I avoid annoying Blayre by having a predictable process that she has learned to expect with me. I take responsibility for getting my needs met to the best of my ability. I do this because it gives me positive energy which enables me to be more adaptable to her needs. This keeps me centered and calm, and she feels like she comes first and is understood.

I design my world to give me what I need, which gives me more capacity to adapt to give others what they need from me. I have to make choices to create a situation where we both win. To do anything else results in my being annoyed, closed and focused on my needs more than hers. She can't help it, I can. In other words, if I turn into my stressed-out self, our experience together is negatively impacted. I can't control Blayre, but I can strive to understand what works with her and what does not. This is a life skill that I learned at home and apply universally.

Here are a few takeaways: If we don't know who we are and what we need to be motivated, inspired, and centered, it makes it nearly impossible for us to manage ourselves. If we can't manage ourselves, we are minimally effective. When we are minimally effective, we get stressed and act out. Then, who we are being further diminishes our effectiveness and creates negative artifacts (experiences with others and a negative perception of who we are). People remember who we were being and how we impacted them. Eventually we have to go back and dig up the artifacts we created. Usually we spend a lot of time blaming others before we accept accountability. All of this takes time and energy—time and energy we should be spending being effective instead of recovering from the damage done when we act out our stress behavior. Get the picture? Blayre taught me this!

None of the relationships I have with my family would be possible if I had not changed my thinking and, consequently, my behavior. More importantly, my loved ones have been willing to let me out of my self-constructed boxes and accept my changes. However, you will find that getting people to believe you have changed is a much easier task when you have managed the skill of Accountability, which we will discuss in the next chapter.

New Practices 3

The process of getting here and sustaining my brand has not been easy. I bite my lip on many occasions and engage in atonement conversations after slipping up. I constantly fight the temptation to be in denial when I get feedback that does not align with my desired brand. I am not perfect, and I never will be. My satisfaction lies in knowing that I am accepting accountability for my thinking and my actions.

These are the practices that have helped me. I hope that they will help you.
1. Recognize that you are your brand.
2. Do a simple brand assessment. Ask your friends, family, co-workers, boss, direct reports, etc. to tell you the top five to ten words they would use to describe you. At least two items have to reflect opportunities for improvement. Be sure to ask them to define the words they choose. Make sure you pick people who are comfortable with you and will likely be honest with you in their assessment. Proactively seeking feedback and responding to it constructively will increase the quality of the feedback over time.
3. Look inside yourself and define the five universal agreements you want people to have about your brand.
4. Identify the gaps between the information gathered in your brand assessment and your desired brand.
5. Identify the behaviors that you must internalize and embody in order to model your desired brand.
6. Make a list of the people with whom you think you are brand negative, brand positive, and brand neu-

tral. Focus on the brand negative relationships.
7. Determine which of the people with whom you are brand negative will be open to recognize the changes you are prepared to make. Also identify those who will not.
8. Imagine a conversation with the people with whom you are brand negative in which you accept responsibility for your past thinking and behavior and forecast the new thinking and behavior they can expect from you. Don't focus on their behavior that might be impacting you. You haven't yet earned the right to that conversation.
9. Identify the difficulties you might have with this atonement conversation, and what triggers might derail the conversation.
10. Outline a road map that you would use to navigate the conversation. The road map should include:
    - Greeting and opening statement to frame the discussion.
    - A list of the key points you want to cover in the meeting and supporting examples.
    - A request for their perspective on what you are doing to contribute to their negative perception of you.
    - A statement of your commitment.
    - A request to acknowledge improvements when they see them.
    - A request for a meeting 30 to 60 days later to get feedback on how you are doing.
    - A statement of thanks and appreciation for being

able to get the issues out into the open.
11. Here is an example of an atonement conversation:
    - "Thank you for seeing me today, John. I appreciate you taking time out for this meeting. I know that we have not had the best relationship, and I hope that our meeting will be the first step in changing this. My purpose today is to voice my perspective on what I may be doing to contribute to the state of our relationship and to get your perspective as well. Are you okay with having this conversation? (Expect a yes. If you get a no, ask when you can have the conversation with them. If they refuse, you have done what you can do. Move forward with modeling your desired brand and recognize that you just took the first action.)
    - Assuming you got a yes, continue with, "The three things I feel I need to own about the state of our relationship are my lack of collaboration, open communication, and closed mindedness. First, I realize that I have not invited you to our meetings where we make decisions that impact your organization. I acknowledge that on at least three occasions in the last six months our solutions have created problems for you that impact your ability to achieve your goals. Second, I have not shared my thoughts with you about any of our plans for the coming year, which means that, yet again, I am likely to negatively impact you. Third, when you have attempted to bring these things to my attention, I have been unwilling to listen to your

suggestions on how we could improve the process, again resulting in decisions that negatively impact you."
- "Is there anything you would like to add to what I have listed?" (Recognize that your list could be completely wrong but you have opened the channel of communication by demonstrating willingness to accept accountability for your contribution to the state of the relationship. Accept comments and seek clarity and context without being defensive.)
- "I am glad that you have been open with me about your perspectives in addition to those that I have offered. What you can expect from me is… Please recognize that this is a change for me, and I will not be perfect at first, but I am committed to improving our relationship.
- "I have one request of you as I make the changes we have discussed. I would like for you to acknowledge that I am making progress when you see improvement. I am not seeking public acknowledgement, but I am seeking some way of knowing that I am being successful in accomplishing what I have committed to. Can I get your commitment to this?" (Expect a yes and possibly a conversation about how you want to receive the acknowledgement. You should accept a method that is comfortable for them. If you get a no, begin to document for yourself where you have modeled your commitment. Then seek

confirmation from the other party.)
- "I would like to schedule a meeting with you about 60 days out to get feedback on your perception of my performance against the commitments I have made today." (Schedule the session. If they refuse to schedule the session, try again in 30 days or figure out a way to have the conversation informally 60 days out.)
- "Thank you for your time today, John. I am glad we were able to get the issues out on the table and figure out a plan of action to get past this."

Key steps to remember are:
1. Determine a timeline for implementing your desired brand to include atonement conversations.
2. Model your desired brand in a safe environment and work out the kinks before going public—about 60 to 90 days. Remember, this is an inside-out transformation, and your follow-through is critical.
3. Execute your plan, monitor progress, and adjust where necessary. I recommend convening a group of objective individuals who you can use as a sounding board throughout this process.

The Short of it...

As we grow and learn, we will inevitably discover the need to reinvent ourselves and recover from that which we did not know or would not acknowledge about ourselves.

Reflections

Complete the following threads.
1. I need to reinvent myself with…
2. The reason I need to reinvent myself is…
3. In my personal and or professional life, my current brand is causing…
4. In the last 30 to 60 days I have received brand feedback that states…
5. My desired brand is…
6. The benefits of achieving my desired brand are…

"Accept your responsibilities and continue to develop your character. Hold yourself accountable for the conditions you create."

CHAPTER FIVE

Now consciously engaged in his journey, the Traveler anticipated a new opportunity to learn and grow. He remembered the apprehension and fear he felt approaching the previous city, Alignment. These were no longer his feelings as he approached the City of Accountability. Learning and development were now part of his practice.

He called to mind the circumstances he had been born into and the rules and scripts he had learned from the key influencers in his life. Choosing to challenge many of those scripts, the Traveler realized that the questioning techniques the teachers had revealed to him were invaluable guides for his journey. Now he believed that questions were the key to learning; statements had limited his growth because they focused on the known rather than the unknown, what *was* rather than what *could be.*

As he entered the City of Accountability, he noticed that it was the cleanest place he had encountered along his journey. This was especially astonishing given that it was a city with a considerable population. There was no trash on the streets, and everything seemed to sparkle. He wondered how the people managed to keep things so clean. He was surprised to be greeted by a young man, probably a teenager, immediately upon entering the city. The young man was well dressed, enthusiastic, and eager to assist him.

"Greetings. I am called Daniel. How might I best assist you today, sir?" Taken aback by the youthfulness of his new acquaintance, the Traveler took a moment before explaining that he was looking for the Teacher of Accountability.

"I would be happy to escort you to the Teacher's residence."

The Traveler accepted the offer, following Daniel east toward the Teacher's residence. He gave in to his urge to ask his new companion, "How do you manage to keep the city so clean?"

"We all have a role in it, and we gladly contribute, because there is great joy in producing such beauty."

"Who makes sure that everyone does their part?"

"No one. We are each personally responsible for ensuring that we do what we have committed to do. It is our way. The

Teacher will be able to explain it to you."

At the end of their short journey, they arrived at the door of the Teacher's house. Daniel thanked the Traveler for the opportunity to serve him and returned to the gate.

The Traveler knocked on the door and was greeted by a small man trusting the left half of his body to a wooden cane. "Welcome to my home. I have been anticipating your arrival and am very pleased to meet you. My children have told me of their interactions with you, and they compliment you on your learning and growth. My daughter, Sarah, in the City of Reinvention, told me that you are seeking a deeper understanding of accountability. I must admit that this is one of the most difficult concepts to understand, master, and embody. It requires that you maintain a level of consciousness that many reject. It demands great effort. Also, you must understand that accountability is not something to toy with."

"I am not like other travelers. I have journeyed far, and I believe that no goal lies out of my reach. Please tell me, is accountability something that must be embodied at all times? Can I choose to be accountable in one area of my life and a victim in others?"

"You will know. Would you like tea?"

As the two men drank their tea the Traveler remarked, "From all that your family has shared with me, I believe that a sort of continuum exists. There seems to be a progression between Self-Acceptance and Inner Conflict, Alignment and Contradiction, Change and Complacency, and now Accountability and Victim Mentality. As I learn from this family and continue my journey, it appears that I am moving from one end of the continuum toward the other. When I look into the mirror your son gave me, I see myself being more conscious, aligned, and in the process of reinventing myself and moving from being a knower to being a learner. I find that I ask far more questions today than I did when I started my journey, and more frequently than ever I question what I know to be my truth.

"I see the changes in myself, and those who take the time to know me also see the changes. You have said that your children, who have helped me greatly, also see my growth."

"True. Is growth enough?"

"Why wouldn't it be enough?"

"What does all your learning and growth mean if it does not manifest itself in application and increasing levels of accountability for your being and your condition?"

The Traveler knew that through this question the Teacher touched on an important point. "In Accountability one has to accept his responsibilities and continue to develop his character. No one will check to see if we live up to those responsibilities."

The Teacher nodded in agreement. "We find truth in what we do when no one watches. This truth is found in holding ourselves to the high standard of following through on our commitments without making excuses."

The Traveler could see that consciousness and alignment were both at play here. And reinvention comes into play when one takes ownership of not living up to the expectations set with others, or not fulfilling one's commitments. To own reinventing himself with others would mean atoning for not meeting his own standard and taking accountability for creating a situation that may have negatively impacted another person's perception of him. But more importantly, it meant that he must be willing to hold himself accountable for the work it would take to regain trust, confidence, and respect.

Exploring this understanding further, the Traveler mentioned a key idea. "I believe that accountability is something to be embodied at all times and in all areas of one's existence. This is not to say that there are not times when one is a victim. Crimes have victims and children may become victims of the circumstances their parents create. Disease, poverty, and economic disadvantage also produce victims, but we often compound our circumstances and create our own adverse conditions. In the matters of life and the choices we make, we must hold ourselves accountable for the conditions we create for ourselves."

Pleased with his guest's insight, the Teacher responded, "How will you deal with others who do not share your belief?"

The Traveler found himself stumped by this question. He recognized that by believing so strongly in the principle of accountability he was positioning himself to judge others; he knew that this was not his place.

"I guess I could be frustrated by them, avoid them, or attempt to change them. None of which create any value. When someone's lack of accountability impacts me personally, it cannot be acceptable to allow it to get in the way of what I am trying to accomplish. I could set a standard for how we will interact together but that seems to be all about my interests and does not take into consideration the other person's needs. Where it does not personally impact me, I guess it really doesn't matter because that person and those who allow him to not be accountable are the only people impacted."

The Traveler realized that his rambling was not bringing him clarity. "Sir, I must admit that this is the most difficult question I have been asked."

"What is in your domain of influence when dealing with others?"

"Me."

"What is your purpose?"

The Traveler thought to himself that he had heard the question of his purpose before and knew that it was to travel his journey and to help others along the way without imposing his biases and rules upon them. But now he wondered how to balance the expectation of accountability with being unbiased and non-judgmental. He knew that his desire to help others would tempt him to influence others to be more accountable. But he also knew that this was not his place. Suddenly he had his answer.

"My purpose is to help others as I pursue my journey without imposing my biases and without judging. In order to do this, I must be tolerant of others who are different from me because they, too, are on their own journey of discovery. Each person's path is as unique as they are. We have no right to encumber the paths of others. But we reserve our right not to be impeded by them. Each Traveler is at his own stage of development, and some will develop more than others over the course of the journey. Those who recognize they are conflicted, I will direct to the City of Alignment. Those who do not recognize their conflict, I will direct to the City of Consciousness. And I will encourage and befriend those who appear to have lost their way. But I must be careful not to enable them to become victims. Often we do not recognize that we are lost until something happens that brings our condition into our consciousness. At that moment we are ready to learn and choose a path that will reshape our lives. At that moment, we begin to contemplate the connection between our past, present, and future. Only the individual travelers can choose what to keep in their baggage as they continue their journey."

The Teacher looked at the Traveler with pride and amazement, for he could see the Traveler developing before his eyes. He wondered if the Traveler would be strong enough to live up to the standards he was setting for himself. These were new philosophies to live by, and he knew that the Traveler would have a steep learning curve to endure. The Teacher also knew that while it was not easy to change one's thinking, it was quite easy to mimic behavior. He hoped that the Traveler would not be frustrated and tempted to judge and discount others.

"You must visit my sister in the City of Relationship Management. She can help you learn to apply what you have discovered here in your interactions with others. This may help you when you encounter those who do not share your perspectives. Remember, there is something that you can learn from everyone. One does not have to be a Teacher to help you gain valuable insights as you learn and grow. Polarization is the gateway to dysfunction."

For the remainder of the day the Teacher and the Traveler talked of their life experiences. Lunch soon became dinner and before the two men knew it, the time to retire for the evening had come. The Teacher showed the Traveler to his room and embraced him to bid good evening. The Traveler's embrace was reluctant because he so enjoyed their conversation. As he prepared for bed, he wondered what new practices he would need to adopt to help maintain accountability.

The next morning the Traveler and the Teacher had breakfast together before the Traveler started on his journey to the City of Relationship Management. After bidding the Teacher farewell, he picked up his baggage and chose his path. The challenge of his commitment to accountability was heavy on his mind, because he knew that accountability was most often demonstrated through interactions with others. He felt that he spent a lot of time thinking before acting, and he wondered how this would affect his future interactions. Again, his learning left him with more questions and less baggage.

Discussion

About five years ago, I gave a speech, "The Enterprise of One." "Enterprise" focused on the power of managing one's self as an enterprise operating from a strategic plan focused on growth and development. This was before I was exposed to Tom Payne's (1993) book *A Company of One*. I have since read Payne's book, and my interpretation of his work is that at the foundation of creating independence in the workplace is the concept of accountability.

My working definition of accountability is simple. It is the process of taking responsibility for our thinking processes and the choices and conditions that result from our thinking. These choices and conditions extend to both our personal and professional lives. My experience has been that taking ownership of my thinking and the resulting choices and circumstances has empowered me to take action that is within my domain of influence and control. I spend less time blaming and more time considering and accepting my role in creating my conditions. Further, in looking at almost any situation, I can find something that I can improve about my contribution to what's going on that would likely make a positive difference. Notice that I am not talking about "other" here. The emphasis is on me and what I can do to impact how I frame my thinking and experience my world.

Accountability is not about control. It is about motion. It is about recognizing that our thinking and resulting actions can be obstacles to our ability to learn and grow. Imagine that every day you wait for others to change you lose a year of your life. Now imagine that every day you learn, grow, and change adds a year. Don't wait for others to move obstacles in your path. They can't move you and you can't move them in any sustainable way. You have to move out of your own way, which comes from the inside out. It is a cognitive process.

Like the Traveler, we choose the areas of our lives for which we are willing to take accountability, and we choose the areas in which to play victim. As victims, we perceive life as coming at us and not from us. The victim perspective can be convenient because it allows us to shift to someone else the burden of acknowledging a need for change. Once again, we may find ourselves living a sub-optimized life waiting for others to change so that we can move on with our journey. I hope you're not holding your breath!

I have repeatedly found that I am my biggest obstacle. I was encouraged to write this book in 2000. I found every excuse in the world not to. Now that I am finally writing it, I have discovered that I was not ready then. I was the obstacle because my thought process constrained me from taking action. I was encouraged over the years to build more connections with my family. Again, I was not ready. I rationalized away the need, and disconnecting behavior followed. Now I see a direct correlation between my efforts to become more connected and our level of connectedness. In the period that I committed to changing my behavior, the quality of the relationships improved and reciprocity resulted. However, prior to being able to demonstrate a change in behavior, I had to change my thinking. I was also encouraged to be more strategic (long-term) and less tactical (short-term). It took time, but once I gained the strategic focus, my message became much clearer, and my actions quickly aligned with the strategy. No more multifaceted gobbledy-gook. Personal growth and transformation became my *practice* (both as a noun and a verb).

The need to be personally accountable extends from the boardroom to the shanty. Change is possible when we initiate change within ourselves first. Because inconsistency erodes trust and respect, the leader who can't lead himself will likely fail in his attempts to lead others. He has no credibility with followers and has not earned the right to ask of the troops what he has not demonstrated a willingness to do himself. He is not "modeling the way." (Kouzes & Posner, 1995, p. 210-211)

The practice of modeling what we are asking of others is

a necessity. It is at play when we set the example for our children, behave as good neighbors, nurture relationships, build friendships, etc. It is expected. However, what is not visible in these interactions are the thought processes leading to the behavior. Our experience in the City of Consciousness must be ever present in our being if we are to be successful in modeling what we say.

A vivid example is reflected in a recent meeting I had with a business associate. I arranged a meeting to discuss exiting out of two of their accounts. I was unconscious. I walked into the meeting after being immersed in writing this book and forgot to shift gears. What I really wanted was to renegotiate the terms of our relationship, but instead I talked about two accounts, two red herrings that ultimately derailed the whole meeting.

On the way back to my office, I replayed the script of the meeting in my head and was predisposed to blame the other party for the failure of the meeting. The reality was that I was the cause. Here I was writing a book and focusing on a chapter on accountability, yet I was not modeling my writing. I did not sleep well that night. I had not achieved closure.

The next morning I was on a mission. I had spent the evening in conflict with myself, attempting to reframe my perspective. I was finally successful as I got up to begin a new day. I could not write until I resolved my inner conflict. I determined what I needed to own about the situation. All of it!

Over the course of the day I outlined a list of goals that should have been the focus of the discussion in the first place. Nowhere in the list was a reference to the accounts I had previously discussed. I had said that I was focused on partnership, but my words and actions were not consistent with that end. I asked the associate if I could have a "do over." Based on our relationship, he let me off the hook, and we were able to begin where we should have started. Although the overall outcome was less than desirable for both parties, our continued efforts revealed a truth that caused us both to question the viability of continuing the relationship.

The point of this example is that I had to become conscious of my own thinking process and get out of my own way before I could model the proper behavior. I had to reframe my thinking and look at the situation from the perspective of the other parties involved. The interesting part of this was that I knew better. I knew the theoretical foundations, the logic, and the rationale for acting differently, but was not successful in my first attempt.

Evidently, we can know what we should do and still not always be successful in doing it. Being successful requires a constant focus on developing proficiency in not only our practices but also in our thought processes. Argyris and Schön (1974) discuss their ground breaking research on espoused theory of action and theory-in-use in their book *Theory in Practice*.

Imagine an enterprise where leaders, managers, and staff think, act, and communicate in a way that reflects accountability. It would likely be much like the utopia described in this book, where people are consciously committed to their accountabilities and embody thought processes that lead to extraordinary levels of trust, respect, and connectedness within their community.

The people of the City of Accountability have created a

unified story of their existence. Each individual's thought process reflects his story and his role in his own story. The context of the story is not distorted. There is neither ambiguity about what accountability means nor about the thought processes and behaviors that it consistently produces. The environment reinforces demonstrating the behaviors. For each individual, his inner story is his truth, which is supported by his community and makes his story a public story. The result is behaviors consistent with accountability and a sense of commitment to maintaining the purity of the community's shared story. This is a story with a happy ending, but the same dynamic would exist if we were describing the City of Self-Destruction and the story was one that led to a denial of reality.

Actively seeking to understand and challenge thought processes, ensuring alignment, and engaging in open discussion and reflection about what is and what is possible are all elements of learning and growth. Accountability, or owning your contribution to your circumstances, is the way to ensure that you are consistently moving forward, rather than getting stuck in the trap of victim mentality.

Many people misinterpret the concept of accountability. At first glance it looks like you are accepting responsibility when others are unwilling to. This is not so. Instead, you are accepting your contribution to the situation and doing something about it so that you can keep yourself moving forward. This allows you to maintain motion toward your own learning and growth. You remain unstuck and reach your own personal closure. You cannot do this on behalf of another; that is something they must do for themselves. They have to be willing to change their rules and choose to be unstuck.

This is not to say that if someone requests your perspective you should not give it. You should do so in a way that helps them to challenge their own thinking, with questions rather than accusations. This is how they can get themselves unstuck. Remember, we don't know another person's story. They must be willing to reveal it and be willing to challenge it before their transformation can begin. They must make their thinking discussable, and it is not discussable until it is made public. We'll learn more about how to manage our relationships with others in the next chapter.

New Practices 4

The following is a set of practices that I have found to be beneficial as I continue to build my own City of Accountability.

1. Be aware of your story as it relates to accountability.
2. Recognize that your personal story is not a universal truth.
3. Write down five examples of where you have demonstrated accountability within the last 30 days. Go to the people involved and get their perspectives.
4. Identify perception gaps and outline what is contributing to the gaps.
5. Align the feedback with your story and modify your story where necessary. This will require you to challenge your thinking in order to craft a different story.
6. Recognize that changing your thinking takes time and may require you to uncover the source of the thinking first.
7. Use critical questioning techniques to uncover the source of your thinking.

Critical Questioning Techniques

Questions are a vehicle for change. They help us to surface our thinking. I recommend using this technique anytime you are in the process of discovery and attempting to understand a story. You can use it with a note pad sitting across the table from another party or on a whiteboard. You can use it one-on-one or in groups. The value is in getting the involved parties to focus on the thinking rather than the person. The process of using this method helps in the areas of consciousness, alignment, reinvention, relationship management, and reflection.

The following diagram depicts a few of the factors behind the behaviors we choose and the questions that help surface the thoughts and feelings driving the behavior. They are elements of a story. Thinking!

BEHAVIORS

WHAT'S BEHIND BEHAVIOR THINKING?

- ASSUMPTIONS
- BELIEFS
- BIASES
- FEARS
- EXPERIENCES

USE QUESTIONS TO SURFACE THOUGHTS AND FEELINGS

1. What do you think about the recent changes?
2. Do you expect that they will affect you?
3. How do you feel about that?
4. Do you have a strategy for how you will deal with that?
5. What level of support do you expect from your sponsors?
6. I have some ideas that might be helpful. Do you mind if I share them with you?
7. If you do A, how do you see it aligning with your goal of B?
8. How about if you tried Y instead?

PERCEPTIONS OR REALITIES

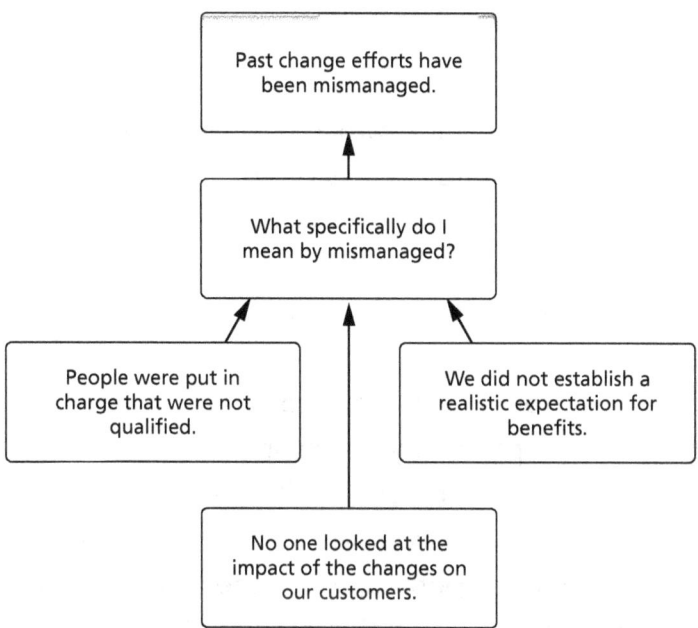

The above diagrams reflect a simulation of the questions and answers resulting from a session to discover the root cause of resistance to a change effort.

Here we see a person's view of why they are resisting a change. Questions 2 and 4 are closed questions that could be revised to be more open-ended as follows:

2. How do you see the changes affecting you?

4. What is your strategy for dealing with the impact on you?

Notice that the statement "Past change efforts have been mismanaged" is an ambiguous statement. "Mismanaged" needs to be clarified. In fact, most of the responses to the questions are likely have elements of ambiguity. Your role in the process is to drill down to clarify meaning as depicted in the following diagram.

Here, the question is clarified further by asking the meaning of "mismanaged."

The farther you drill down the clearer the thinking becomes. As the facilitator of this discovery process, you help get to the essence of the story with the goal of identifying gaps, inconsistencies, flawed logic, etc. that will help the person challenge his own story. You are facilitating a breakthrough.

While this process is difficult to break down into specific questions that apply in any circumstance (since the individual questions are so situation-specific), you can see from the above list that the questions are open-ended and designed to elicit a range of responses, which then lead to more questions. Starting with a general framework that includes questions like, "What do you think of…?", "How do you feel about…?", "What do you expect of…?" and "What has been your experience with…?", you will be able to dive deeper and deeper into the participants' thought processes and uncover the root of any problems. The key is to listen without judgment, and to seek a full understanding of the thinking behind the behavior. Your true goal, like the Teachers in the story, is to lead the other party to find their own breakthrough, not to lecture them about the breakthrough you believe they should have. I have discovered that I often have not been fully conscious of why I was responding to a situation in a particular way. This technique has helped me surface and scrutinize my own thinking as well. If you plan to use this technique with others, it's a good idea to use it on yourself first and discover any hidden agendas or undiscovered motives. Talking about your own discoveries might also help others at the table feel more comfortable disclosing their own thoughts and feelings. A good leader leads by example.

The Short of it...

We have to accept our responsibilities and continue to develop our character. We must hold ourselves accountable for the circumstances we create for ourselves.

Reflections

Complete the following threads.
1. I feel I should be accountable when...
2. I demonstrate accountability when...
3. The feedback I have received in the last 30 days about my demonstration of accountability states...
4. I have the most difficulty demonstrating accountability when...
5. Examples of people I know who are accountable include_____. They model accountability by...
6. The benefits of increasing my accountability are...

"Communicating in a way that increases the level of connectedness between individuals and within teams, fosters opportunities for knowledge creation, learning, and personal growth."

CHAPTER SIX

The terrain between the City of Accountability and the City of Relationship Management was more rugged than the Traveler had experienced before. Rather than consisting of rocks and soil, the Traveler found himself managing a trail that also included streams and significant sloping grades. And this wasn't the first mountainside segment of his journey. Something was different.

The journey required the Traveler to expend a great deal of energy, so he decided to stop for rest. He came across a shade tree where he tried to relax, but his attention continually returned to the relationships he had in the past and his role in the success and failure of those relationships. He also thought about how past relationships influenced his behavior in new relationships. He was inclined to spend more time thinking about the successes than the failures, but he forced himself to focus more on the failures. This exercise demanded much of his thought energy, but it certainly afforded him time for his body to regroup. He decided, finally, to hop back onto the trail.

He thought about the conflicts and arguments he had engaged in and realized that there were several phrases that he seemed to use consistently whenever he became engaged in conflict. "If you would..." "Your problem is..." "I am not the one who..." "This is the last time I am going to..." "I am fed up with..." "If you do this to me again..." "You must think I..."

Given that accountability was salient in his mind after visiting that fair city, he found no evidence of the practice of accountability in his own behavior. Still, the most disturbing revelation was that he used the same phrases in the interactions he considered successful. The difference was that in the successful interactions, the other people allowed him to talk to them that way. In those he perceived as failures, the other person always pushed back. He thought that maybe he confused his definitions of success and failure. After more thought, he realized his definitions were not backwards, but he sorely needed to change his conflict behavior. While he was able to arrive at this conclusion, he was unable to identify any options for what his conflict behavior should look like. The looming question became, "Change to what?"

Noticing that his pace had slowed considerably, the Traveler decided to make haste, still wrestling with his thoughts about these past interactions. After a few more miles, it occurred to him that his conversations with the teachers were much different. They were collaborative, and he listened to them and respected their perspectives. They were like trusted advisors with whom he could be open and share his innermost feelings. He thought about a possible connection there, between his views of them and the interactions they shared, but he concluded nothing. His thoughts floated back to his perceptions of his interactions with others and how he could take more ownership of his communications, especially when the communications dealt with conflict or disagreement. He had no immediate answers.

The Traveler struggled with his questions as he progressed in this leg of his journey. The City of Relationship Management couldn't be too far ahead, he thought, so he generated a list of questions he wanted to ask the Teacher. However, from past experience he knew that the Teacher would most likely present a completely different set of questions for him to ponder. As he neared the city, he passed others who were leaving, possibly en route to other destinations. From his view, they were really engulfed in their conversations, appearing to have genuine interest in whatever was their subject. He decided to listen in, and in doing so he noticed that they questioned much more than they declared. Even their responses seemed unusual. He heard phrases such as "Tell me more about...," "How might we...," "What would be another...," "If we were to...," "How does this align with...," "I never knew that...," and "What is contributing to...."

Because he was unable to hear full conversations, the Traveler decided to stop, rest, and listen in the courtyard at the city entrance. He was fascinated by the conversations he heard. In each case, he noticed the same phenomenon—each person was intent on connecting in such a way that the other was heard and felt understood. This seemed so easy for them to do, and it appeared that each had internalized some type of standard practice. They seemed to expect this type of interaction from each other. He could manage no response except to wonder, "How does this all come so easily to them?"

After spending hours in the courtyard, the Traveler asked a young woman where he could find the Teacher of Relationship Management. "Our brother is in the Garden of Engagement. You can find it just at the top of the stairs nearest the river."

The Garden of Engagement was only a short distance from the courtyard. The Traveler made his way to the garden, where a middle-aged man who closely resembled the Teacher of Accountability—maybe a little taller but definitely with better posture—greeted him.

The Traveler told the Teacher of the interactions he observed on his way into the city, especially what he saw in the courtyard. "My friend, I am not surprised. This is simply the way of our culture."

"How can people communicate this way? There is something unnatural about it. They continually ask questions of one another."

"What did you hear? What did you see?" the Teacher asked.

The Traveler was surprised at these questions since he just explained to the Teacher what he had seen and heard. "Do you mean beyond what I have already told you?"

"Yes."

"I think I saw people who were really interested in what other people had to say, and I believe what I did not hear were phrases that brought about defensiveness or divisiveness."

"Yes. What you saw was what was on the outside. What you could not see was what was going on inside or what was influencing them. You could not see what the two people were committed to. You could not see the environmental factors that helped them to communicate in the way you observed. Anyone can model what you have seen and observed, but why is it that you have seen little of this before entering this city? What do you know about this culture?"

The Traveler was embarrassed to know so little about the history of this city. He had not inquired into their culture before leaving the City of Accountability. He admitted his ignorance to the Teacher, who then shared with him the history and culture of the people there.

The Teacher told the Traveler a story about the original founders of the city. "Two exploration parties from two different cultures arrived here on the same day. They met at the very location of the courtyard where you observed those interactions upon your arrival in the city. These two cultures had very different customs and beliefs. However, because neither was accustomed to the climate and the land there, they found it necessary to share knowledge and work together to survive and prosper. Over time, the two groups united, and other members from the two cultures moved in. They all worked together to build the city. Over the years the two cultures blended into the culture that lives and thrives here today. Everyone you see in our society has blood colored by many different experiences and cultures. No one has blood that is completely pure and without the history and strengths of others."

After sharing this story, the Teacher asked, "How do you think the two cultures came together without bigotry or prejudice?"

"Maybe they needed each other to survive?"

"You do not seem sure of this possibility. Tell me, how do you think they came to trust each other?"

To this the Traveler answered, "I don't think they did at first, but of course I don't know. I would guess that they made promises or set expectations with one another and waited to see if they lived up to their commitments. It could be that they were curious about each other and wanted to learn more and learned to appreciate their differences. Another possibility is that each culture was already experienced in dealing with a wide variety of other cultures, so this was their way. My last thought is that somehow they were not afraid and believed that if they treated each other with dignity and respect, they would receive the same in return."

The Teacher smiled and said, "Your insights are impressive. The truth is, at first they did none of those things. They were suspicious and wary of relying on each other. But soon their attempts at self-sufficiency failed, and they discovered that they each needed some knowledge or skill that the other culture possessed. In their hour of need, our ancestors realized they had two choices: mistrust their new companions and struggle to make do in an environment of fear and suspicion, or put aside their fears and thrive in this new land by getting to know one another and appreciating each other's contributions. Once they made their choice, creating a culture in which curiosity about each other overruled judgment and fear was a matter of keeping their everyday choices aligned with the overall goal of collaboration and openness. Our way is simple. We strive to help each other in our journeys without judgment. We are sincere in our efforts to understand others and to understand what we can do to make our lives better together. We do not always agree and we do not always produce the best outcomes when we have disagreement, but we do strive to reach the best possible outcome given the situation. Foremost in our minds is to avoid harming each other by saying things that we can't take back. If we are angry, we disengage before we say or do something that is not reversible. We look at ourselves and evaluate what we are doing to contribute to the situation at hand, and we hold ourselves, and each other, accountable. This is our culture." Accentuating the word culture, the Teacher paused briefly before continuing.

"When we find a person who is not being accountable, we use questions to help uncover the nature of their struggle, and we collaborate to find solutions that others can live with. Sometimes one party in the interaction has to work harder than the other. It would be easy to keep score of this, but that would prove fruitless, maybe even self-defeating. And we refuse to be defeated.

"We are committed to giving to the situation all that we

can, purely because we have the capacity to do so. And on the days when our capacities are low, we hope that the other party can make up the difference. Sometimes we recognize that no good can be produced in the present moment, so we defer to another day. The key here is that we have a choice, and in most cases we get more than we give. This is our way. This is what is inside us. It is all possible because our belief is that we are all committed to each other, and we trust and respect each other. Lastly, we are committed to rebuilding trust and respect when it is broken. We are committed to forgiveness. To what are you committed?"

Again, the Traveler was speechless. This culture still seemed very unnatural to him. "I'm struggling to understand how the people have developed these skills." "It is simple. You must resist the urge to complicate it." The Traveler was beginning to feel frustrated by what he perceived as a circular conversation. "Do you mean that it is as simple as making a commitment?"

"Absolutely not."

"Well, do you mean that it is about committing to creating the environment, committing to the people you deal with, and committing to the practices?"

"Can you do that?"

"I guess it would depend on who the other party is and the importance of the relationship to me." The Traveler was beginning to see some promise in his tireless mental efforts.

"And what of those people whom you deem unimportant?" The Teacher knew that his guest could go farther.

The Traveler had an epiphany. "As I learned in the City of Accountability, it is an all or nothing commitment. I am either a person who cares about others and communicates with all people in a way that reflects this, or I am a person that cares about himself and communicates in a way that will result in only me getting what I want. This appears to describe another continuum. I am committed to operating on the end of the continuum that models being committed to others as much as I can."

To this the Teacher said, "No one can ask for more than this from you."

The Traveler thought that this was both truly simple and difficult to embody. He felt that it would take a great deal of practice for him to develop this skill from the inside out, but he acknowledged that there was merit in doing so. He wanted to be able to engage others through interaction, and he also wanted to be able to model the practices he observed. He believed this would be a tall order for him to fill and that it would be impossible if he did not truly commit to both an internal transformation and an outward change in his practices.

The Teacher invited the Traveler to stay with him for the evening. He agreed, but he also wanted to spend some time alone thinking about what he had just learned. He had to consider this in light of the lessons taught to him by all of his previous teachers.

They walked to the Teacher's home where dinner was waiting. While they ate the Traveler told the Teacher about his visits with the Teacher's relatives and the progress he was making in applying what he had learned in his life. He also shared how grateful he was to have such wonderful coaches to help him on his journey. He admitted that he was lost until they came into his life and that he now looked forward to the challenges before him. He also wondered if he would ever again become lost.

"Only you can determine this. However, my sister in the City of Reflection may be able to help you with this question. I am sure by the time you arrive there you will have several other questions for her as well."

After dinner the Traveler and the Teacher walked through a garden near his home. The two men walked for a long while, and the Teacher told more stories about the city and the culture of the people who lived there. The Traveler then asked about the culture of the people in the City of Reflection and about the history of the city. The Teacher shared with him that the people there were highly evolved and communicated in a way very similar to the people in his city. He went on to describe how the people were able to analyze the impacts of their behavior as they were engaged in it. This practice fascinated the Teacher, and hearing about it encouraged the Traveler. At the conclusion of their walk, the Traveler felt that he would be entering the city with at least a basic knowledge of the people and their culture, and he retired to his room for the evening.

The next morning the Traveler prepared to leave for the City of Reflection. He thought about ways to internalize the communication practices he had learned here in the City of Relationship Management.

He no longer concerned himself with making accommodations for being unfamiliar with his hosts, so he resisted the urge to find out the name of his next teacher. Besides, he was finding that the journey was enough without the need to label everyone he met. He realized he had never asked the name of his current acquaintance either. Excited to continue on his journey, he picked up the tiny bundle that now represented his baggage and found the path toward his new destination.

Discussion

Our relationships with others can be viewed as the landscape of our lives, and we spend our whole existence tending to it (or in some cases, neglecting it). In some periods of our lives divorce, death, feuding, marriage, new birth, and reconciliation drastically change the landscape. Who we are has a significant impact on the health and quality of our relationships. How we communicate can be viewed as a manifestation of who we are.

The way we deal with situations that challenge who we are provides a window into the essence of our beings. We choose what end of the continuum we want our reaction to align with. Our responses will lie near the defensive end of the spectrum or near the open end. What is important to note is that we choose our reactions and our methods either consciously or unconsciously.

The Traveler was fascinated by the way the people of the City of Relationship Management communicated. It was markedly different from his practice. He learned that a combination of internal and environmental factors led people to behave as he observed. The people were able to put themselves in a state where they were genuinely interested in the perspectives of others. It was a part of who they were as individuals, and it was reflective of their culture.

The key questions of the Traveler include: How did these practices come to exist? Was it because of their ancestors? If so, how did their ancestors become enlightened? Could the behavior exist in an environment that did not support it? Why did the people continue to choose to adopt these practices generation after generation?

What are the answers? The answers to the Traveler's questions are much like the answers to our inquiries. That is, we must learn to increase our effectiveness, our level of connectedness, the quality of our relationships, and the quality of our communications. The benefits are better results through increased understanding, teamwork, and collaboration.

LaFasto and Larson (2001) address the factors that make good team members in their book *When Teams Work Best*. They found trusting, caring, helpful, open, honest, and respectful among the words participants in their study used to describe the best relationships they had with team members (LaFasto and Larson, 2001, p 37). They found unreasonable, unfair, selfish, threatening, and inflexible to be among the words used to describe the worst relationships (LaFasto and Larson, 2001, p 37). They also found good relationships to be constructive, productive, self-corrective, and characterized by mutual understanding (LaFasto and Larson, 2001, p 37 – 38). Each of these characteristics is a reflection of communication through words and actions.

Obviously communication is a complex act, but it is reflective of what we think. Below is a model that represents this. The model depicts that behind our communication are goals, fears, beliefs, biases, etc. This is not an exhaustive list. The model also represents that these forces impact the perception of the other person and their personal brand. Ultimately, it impacts the quality of the relationships we manage through our communications.

NEGOTIATING MEANING

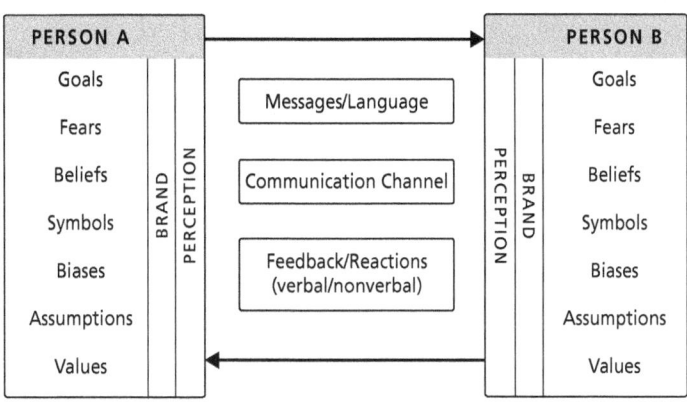

ADAPTATION OF THE CONSTRUCTIVIST MODE

In each relationship that makes up the landscape of our lives, our personal brand is present. My position is that our personal brand influences how others perceive us through our communication acts. Consequently, if we are brand negative with others, they are likely to perceive our communications in line with their negative connotation of who we are. The same applies with those with whom we are brand positive.

However, how we communicate impacts how we are perceived. That perception and our brand are somewhat synonymous.

The following diagram reflects the pressure that surrounds our interactions with others. In many cases we may not be conscious of these pressures, while in other cases they literally stand in front of us.

138 THINK!

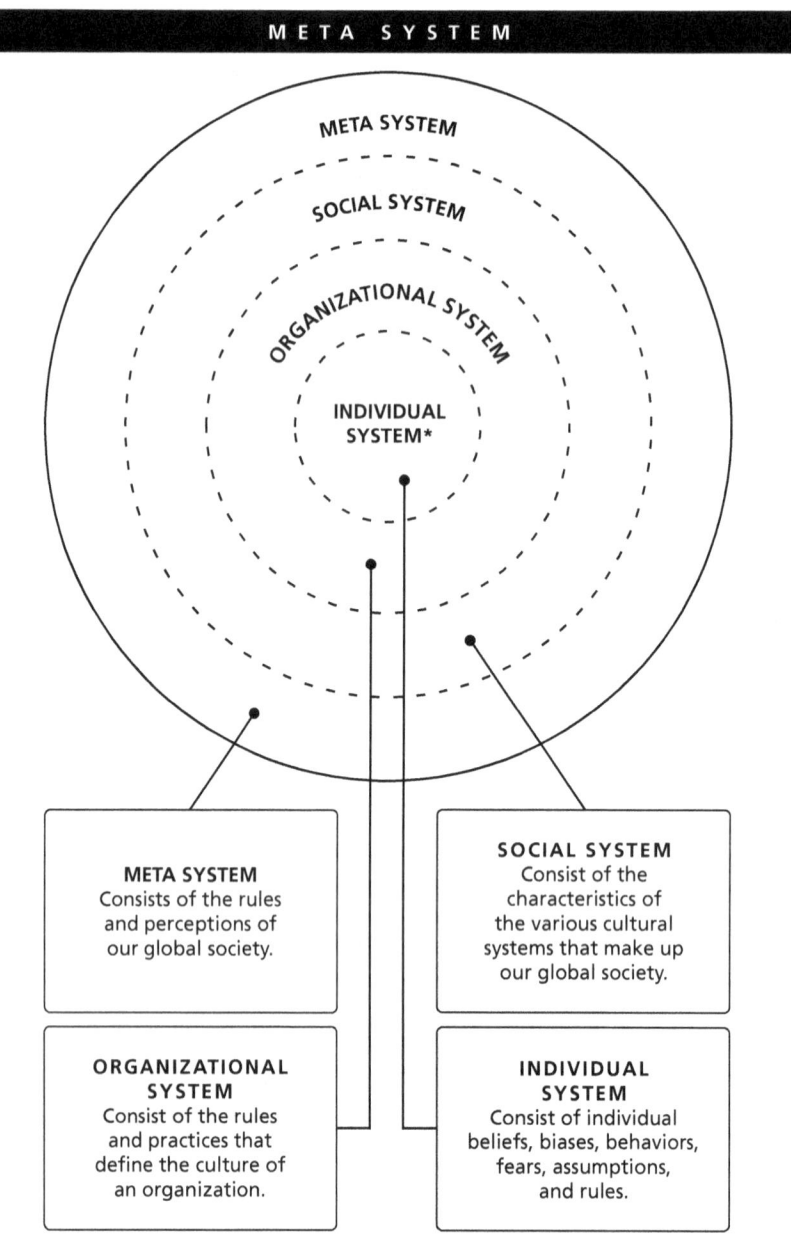

*Individual Systems manifest themselves in individual to individual interactions and/or relationships.

As you view this diagram, imagine that the force is from the outside in and that invisible forces are being exerted on every personal and professional interaction you have. The source of the pressure could be economic, social, cultural, religious, etc. Our ability to effectively navigate our interactions may depend on our ability to understand others and how they perceive us. Make the self-talk public.

The Traveler observed a culture in which demonstrating genuine interest in others was both practiced and valued. Understanding each other's perspectives, thought processes, thinking, feelings, assumptions, etc. was a priority, and, more importantly, a part of learning. There was genuine interest in developing new understanding and new knowledge. From that knowledge new meaning was derived that enhanced the quality of the communications.

Can you and/or your organization benefit from new learning? Do your current communication practices enhance your ability to connect with others and gain or create new meaning? What are the potential benefits? What's missing?

It starts with you. What about your communication practices help and hinder you from connecting with others? What opportunities are lost when the connection is not made? What about your way of communicating causes you to get in your own way? What are you willing to change about your thinking in the next 30 to 60 days that will increase your ability to connect with others? How will you know the change has occurred?

What has helped me connect with others is that I love learning about people, and I enjoy finding out why others think what they think and do what they do. I like asking questions rather than making statements. I do make statements of my perspective and what has worked for me, but only after asking several questions to gain the other person's perspective and context. I have found that I learn much more when I ask why, what and how.

Remember that effective relationship management starts with you. If you are consistently practicing the skills of consciousness, alignment, reinvention, and accountability, and you refrain from judging others who are on a different journey from you, then the pathway to healthy relationships is well mapped out. One more skill, that of Reflection, will help you keep tabs on how you are doing in all these areas, so that you can continue a lifelong journey of growth and discovery.

New Practices 5

This book provides you with a perspective, but you are left to define your own journey and to customize your own toolset. I have provided you with starters and examples of what has worked for me, but you have to complete the construction by asking yourself the questions that lead to your answers to why, what and how. Own your journey.

The following are some of the practices that have helped me improve my effectiveness in managing relationships.
1. Don't strive to be right, but to be curious.
2. Listen to learn. Don't judge, but instead focus on understanding the other person's why, what, and how. Genuine interest gains more disclosure and an opportunity to gain greater context.
3. Ask meaningful questions, but don't make it an inquisition.

4. Strive to understand context and overcome ambiguity.
5. Recognize that people have reasons for doing what they are doing, but they may not know what they are yet. They also may not be conscious of what they are doing. Don't assume that their actions are deliberate.
6. Understand that the situation and the environment impact the quality of communication.
7. Recognize that two of the benefits of making a connection are better solutions and better results.
8. Don't take away someone's voice. Everyone wants to be heard.
9. Create a space conducive to connecting.

Using these steps, you are likely to learn things that you never knew before about what is getting in the way of effective relationships, employee engagement, innovation, and more.

The Short of it...
Communicating in a way that increases the level of connectedness between individuals and within teams fosters opportunities for knowledge creation, learning, and personal growth.

Reflections

Complete the following threads.
1. My personal and professional relationships are...
2. The people I have relationships with personally and/or professionally would characterize our relationship as...
3. My idea of an effective personal and/or professional relationship is...
4. I have an easier time establishing and maintaining relationships with people who...
5. Examples of a connected relationship that I have with others include...
6. The levels of connectedness in my relationships are in place because...
7. The feedback I have received lately relating to my professional and/or personal relationships is...

"Reflection is the pathway to learning and reinvention."

CHAPTER SEVEN

Armed with the information he had gained about the culture and the people of the City of Reflection, the Traveler made his way there. On his mind were haunting questions: How could anyone be self-monitoring in a real-time fashion? What does it really mean to be self-monitoring, anyway? What does that look like? What steps do they take to achieve such consistent self-awareness? He was eager to see this behavior for himself. He did not know that reaching the city would take much more time than he anticipated.

Although it was taking the Traveler much longer to reach the city than he foresaw, he determined not to rush his journey. Instead, he made his way through many villages and took advantage of opportunities to practice the communication skills he had learned. He felt that he was truly transforming himself from the inside out. The more he was able to empathize with others, the more natural modeling the practices became.

The Traveler also spent a great deal of time attempting to become self-monitoring in his communications with others. The villages he crossed presented prime opportunities to practice monitoring his responses in the different interactions he had. Nonetheless, he found the practice difficult to manage. How could anyone connect with another person and also be self-monitoring in the interaction? When he was able to monitor his thoughts and feelings, he was not connecting, and when he was connecting he was not self-monitoring. He could do only one or the other. He had no idea how to fully see himself while seeing another person. Regardless, he was determined not to give up, so he continued to practice.

After devoting a tremendous amount of time to engaging the idea of self-monitoring, the Traveler thought that he might not have understood truly what the Teacher of the City of Relationship Management meant by the people being able to analyze the impact of their behavior as they engaged in it. He thought the Teacher meant the impact of their communications, but could he have been indicating that the people were able to understand the impact of their situational behavior on their ability to accomplish their goals? Isn't all behavior communicating something?

The Traveler was more lost now than ever and in desperate need of answers. He became more determined to reach the City of Reflection. He now knew that the learning he would experience there would be key to his journey.

The Traveler continued to think about what Reflection really meant and remained eager to get answers. Finally arriving at the city gates, he was greeted, to his surprise, by the Teacher of Reflection. As the Teacher ushered him into the city, the Traveler noticed that many people were walking alone, seemingly with a distinct purpose. Everyone he saw appeared focused intently on reaching whatever destination they had.

The Traveler asked the Teacher, "Why is it that these people travel alone?"

"Are you not traveling alone as well?"

This had not occurred to the Traveler when he asked his question. He was so busy watching others that he did not recognize the behavior that he projected.

"They walk alone because they choose to," the Teacher explained.

"Do the people of your city ever travel together?"

"Of course. Have you not traveled alone and also with others at various times along your journey?" Again the Traveler had lost sight of the connection between what he modeled what he observed.

Twice now the Teacher's questions had provided the Traveler with awakening experiences. This got his attention, and he decided that he would now think before he asked another question of the Teacher. When he felt confident again, the Traveler asked, "Where are we going?"

"We are going to the Graveyard of Complacency. Through it runs the River of Learning. We will take my boat down the River of Learning to my home, the Palace of Actualization, where I host many Travelers."

"How long do your guests stay in the Palace?"

"Most stay only a short time, but there are a few who have been with me for many years," answered the Teacher.

"Will I be there for long?"

"Only you can determine this. I don't mean to scare you, but several travelers are buried here in the Graveyard of Complacency."

"How do they die?" The Traveler grew more and more uneasy with the prospect of not reaching total success.

"When these travelers left the Palace of Actualization, they wandered for years and returned here to die. I would say they died from a lack of purpose. They achieved great things in their lives, but they stopped growing. They became complacent, and most fell into ruin of one sort or another. This is why we call it the Graveyard of Complacency."

The Traveler was surprised that the Teacher of Relationship Management had not mentioned this to him. The Teacher went on to describe the relationship between the Graveyard of Complacency, the River of Learning, and the Palace of Actualization. She explained that many travelers were seeking opportunities to apply their talents, and in this pursuit they set goals for themselves that are often linked to titles, money, or recognition. As they accomplish these goals, incrementally, they become actualized. For many, however, the actualization is only temporary because the travelers become complacent with their accomplishments and often cease to do the things that led them there, or they do not recognize that their thinking needs to continue to change as the world around them changes. "Over time, they lose the energy to navigate the River of Learning, which led them to The Palace of Actualization in the first place.

"For those who have made a home in the Palace of Actualization, they have learned to anticipate complacency. They have learned to be in tune with the feelings associated with becoming comfortable, entitled, and having stories geared more toward their past than what they are accomplishing at the present, with an eye toward the future. They have learned to pave their own paths and master their lives from the inside out. No longer are they influenced by a mediated definition of success. They define their own successes, a fundamental component of which is growth, complemented by an extraordinary ability to be reflective. The measure of their growth is not in the titles, the wealth, and the recognition they attain. Their growth is measured by their ability to be reflective and make breakthrough improvements within themselves that translate into making an impact in the lives of others. They march to their own beat and are committed to excellence, continuous learning and inner growth."

By the time the Teacher finished this explanation, the Traveler was intent on becoming a resident of the Palace of Actualization. However, he knew he was not ready because he had not mastered the practice of reflection. "How can I master the practice of reflection?" he asked the Teacher.

"You must learn to make time to think and to contemplate that which you must master about yourself. You must establish a practice of voluntarily putting yourself in situations where you are forced to see yourself through a different lens so that you may identify new growth opportunities. The rest you must determine for yourself, for only you can know what you specifically need to enable yourself. One size does not fit all."

The Teacher and the Traveler reached the edge of the River of Learning. They boarded the Teacher's boat and made their way toward the palace. The Traveler was still challenged by how he would develop his skills of reflection.

They arrived at the Palace of Actualization and were greeted by many of the travelers residing there. The number of people there amazed the Traveler. He thought to himself that so many travelers had made their way there, and they represented all genders, races, religions, and abilities. However, he could not help wondering which travelers would not be there the next day. He hoped that he would be there.

The Teacher led the Traveler to his room within the palace and gave him some time to get settled in and mingle with the other travelers. The woman who occupied the next room, Ruth, had been a resident of the palace for many years. To the Traveler, Ruth appeared to be about his age. He made his way to her room, curious about her length of stay in the palace. After they introduced themselves, he asked her the question that was burning in his mind.

She explained that in her early years she was constantly in and out of the palace. Each time that she thought she had figured out the practices that would keep her there, she found herself leaving the palace.

The Traveler asked what her Transformation Point was, and she explained that there were many Transformation Points. "And I continue to have them today."

Ruth went on with what was to her a story, although it seemed to the Traveler to be more of a lesson. Nonetheless, with great conviction and detail Ruth discussed her series of attempts to remain in the palace. She told of how she learned to put together a plan for her development, learning, and growth. She described to the Traveler how she frequently assessed herself in different areas of her growth and convinced others to do the same. "After attempting to assess my growth alone, I realized that I was fruitful only when I've accepted the assessments of others. Now, I use the assessments of others to reconcile my own."

"It sounds like you've got a really static process that you follow."

"Then I reflect on the feedback I receive and outline an Action Plan for improving. My plan includes my specific goals and timelines and the support resources I need in order to succeed. At times, I become so focused on growing that I may go so far as to document conversation scripts to help with difficult conversations. I normally utilize this when I have to go and atone, forecast, and reinvent myself with other travelers."

Ruth continued, describing her goal of Personal Branding. She routinely compiled a list of the five things she wanted to be synonymous with hearing her name or seeing her face. "I know that as the occasional subject of travelers' discussions, my brand can be present when I cannot."

Ruth also explained that her Action Plan was linked to her Personal Brand; she knew that if she executed her plan she increased the level of alignment between her actions and the Personal Brand she wanted to embody. The final point Ruth discussed was the link between her Action Plan and her ability to be reflective.

Her words gave the Traveler a verbal timeline: once she internalized her Action Plan and believed in the results to which she committed, it was easier to be aware of the thinking that needed to change in order to produce the behaviors she wanted to model in her interactions with others. Ruth believed that her communications practices and actions had to align with her Personal Brand and that the more she practiced the less time she had to spend being self-monitoring in her interactions. Ruth did make a point to clarify that she was not one hundred percent connected with others when she communicated with them because some portion of her attention had to be reserved for self-monitoring activities. However, that percentage of time spent self-monitoring declined as she became more proficient and aligned. Like the other skills the Traveler had learned on his journey, the practice of Reflection, too, was like learning to ride a bicycle.

The Traveler was enlightened and asked Ruth if she thought the process would work for him. He felt relieved to have a chance to contribute a few of his own thoughts.

Ruth explained that most of the travelers that managed to remain in the palace for an extended time had adopted some version of this practice. This revelation gave the Traveler new confidence in his potential to remain in the palace. He also knew he would likely have to leave a few times before he was proficient. The Traveler asked, "Does using this process put you at risk for becoming complacent if you find success with it?"

"It does if you don't routinely evaluate how your process

can be improved. For example, it took me years to develop the different components of my practice. The only way I found out that more was required was by routinely asking myself what was possible. I routinely change the questions in my assessment and ask others what questions they would add. I have also found that I navigate toward the people who are likely to provide me with critical feedback instead of those who will tell me only positive things. I pay special attention to feedback that tells me how I am improving in the areas outlined in my Action Plan."

The Traveler thanked Ruth for sharing her practices with him and asked if they could talk more. Ruth graciously volunteered to make herself available to him for coaching.

The Traveler returned to his room excited about the new friend he had made and began to think about the questions he could formulate to assess where he could improve. He quickly made his way back to Ruth's room to ask if she would share the questions she used for her last assessment. She was happy to give him the list. He reviewed them and made several adjustments to tailor it for his own use. As he started toward his door, he heard a knock. It was Ruth. She said that she had failed to share one of her practices with him. She went on to explain that one could easily get lost in practicing methodology and lose sight of the heart of the matter. In her experience, remaining in the Palace of Actualization was a blend of head and heart, and to truly be effective he would need to tap into the source of his emotions to find objectivity. He attempted to ask her questions to gain more context, but her only response was that he would have to find his own answers, his unique truth. He was puzzled but accepted her response. When she left he sat in his room for a long time trying to find the meaning in her words.

After a long while, the Traveler went to the Teacher of Reflection to discuss what he had learned from Ruth. The Teacher was pleased to see that his guest had wasted no time in seeking out the resources he would need to improve his chances of a long stay in the palace. Still, the Traveler had much to learn. For one, he had not yet mastered the practice of sitting still in deep reflection.

Discussion

Imagine meeting someone like Ruth who is willing to share all of her experiences, practices, and wisdom with you freely and with no expectation of anything in return. Guess what? You can give this gift to yourself each and every time you engage in reflection.

My working definition of reflection is taking time to think about where we are in our journeys, how we got there, who are we being, and what is possible for the future. It provides us with the opportunity to be at rest instead of constantly in motion. It is also an opportunity to discover what should be the next phase of our journey. It is a time to design our next reinvention.

For six years we lived in a hundred-year-old Victorian home. We purchased it from a couple, both musicians. They had completely renovated the home themselves. It was beautiful, and they took care to maintain the integrity of the home.

A few years later there was a knock on the door. Two siblings, who were the offspring of the home's original owners, had come by to visit the home. I walked through the house with them, and they began to tell me stories of events that had happened in each of the rooms of the house and how the house had been changed ever so slightly over the years. At the end of the tour and their continual outpouring of gratitude for letting them visit, they handed me the original closing documents from their purchase of the house. This was an unexpected but meaningful experience. They were retracing their journey.

When I reflect on my journey, it reminds me of the freeways of Houston, Texas—always under construction! In my adult life, my first reinvention was from boy to man in the Air Force. The next was from Airman to front-line supervisor in a communications company. I have gone from being a management engineer to an author, speaker, consultant, and coach. These are reinventions related to what I do. That's easy. Many people can do this.

The hard work is on the inside, surfacing the stories in your head that lead to your choices and reimagining them in ways that lead to more effective decision-making. Note that I am not referring to your internal wiring (your motivational needs), but to the thinking and rules that shape your worldview and your actions. This kind of transformation takes longer, and it is something that many don't do. You get to choose which end of the continuum you want to be nearest. Do you choose to be constantly improving or in complacency? Why?

Remember that you are writing your own story with your thoughts, actions, and inactions. You are the only thing standing in your way. What will it take for you to move and sustain your motion? What is your personal action plan? What are you waiting for? There is a plot waiting for you in the Graveyard of Complacency should you choose to occupy it. THINK! about it!

The Traveler recognized that he had to overcome the temptation of complacency in order to reach actualization. He also learned that the temptation to be complacent about his learning and growth would always be there. It would tempt him to settle for where he was on his journey instead of stretching himself to take advantage of greater learning and opportunities. The Traveler also recognized that the enemy of actualization was complacency. Success may not necessarily produce more success. However, success may produce complacency. Think about it!

The more successful we become, the more our story reinforces the behavior that created the success. Why would you question your practices if they produced the results you sought? The real questions become, "Are you as effective as you could be? What is possible for you? What unintended consequences may have been created that you have conveniently dismissed?" You likely don't know the answers. This provides an opportunity to revel in our success while also thinking about what could bring even greater success. This does not mean that you have to actively pursue greater outward success. It means that you should understand what will be necessary to maximize your inner success.

The world around us is in a constant state of motion. This motion inadvertently is making old practices obsolete. The challenge we face is anticipating what will continue to make us viable assets in a changing world. This is where we have to make reflection work for us and not against us. Looking inward without a context of what is going on around us is self-defeating. We should go inward in order to be more effective in mapping our journey in a world that is ever-changing. In a global environment this is essential. Otherwise we will find ourselves with jobs in dying industries that have been dying before our eyes for years, but we react as though it started only yesterday. We find ourselves ill-prepared to adapt. We claim victim when we should have claimed action.

Ruth takes initiative to understand where she is with her brand, but she also takes time to gather perspectives on what is on the horizon so that she can properly prepare. She is reflective, and she is proactive. She is actively taking careful stock of what she needs to embody in order to achieve her goal of remaining actualized. Ruth has not left it to someone to come and tell her that she is underperforming. She has taken accountability for her thoughts and actions. Ruth is growing. Ruth is successful but not complacent. She is learning. Ruth is living her love for herself, and that love of self is reflected in her willingness to help others.

Ruth reengineers her toolkit. She continually evolves her tools to increase her effectiveness. She shares her tools with others in hopes that they, too, will achieve their goals. Ruth sees the reflection in her mirror, and she sees her truth. When she shares that mirror with others, her truth is reaffirmed. As a result, Ruth is engaging and reshaping her world one encounter at a time. I imagine Ruth could accomplish just about anything she set her mind to, and would be an effective leader in any organization. Ruth knows how to get to the heart of the matter for her. Your challenge is to find the way to get to the heart of what really matters to you!

New Practices 6

Ruth spelled out her process in detail to the Traveler. The following is a list of practices that have helped me in the reflection process.
1. Spend an hour each day reflecting. Pick a time that is convenient and a space that is conducive. My secret is to turn on a Western. For some reason it relaxes me, and I can immediately engage in reflection.
2. Carve out space for yourself that stimulates reflection. I love to sit in outside eating areas, watch other people and think about what their lives might be like. It causes me to think about my life.
3. Spend time with people who like to talk about things they have been thinking about or trying to make sense of. Engage with them to discuss what you are thinking about as well. This can be incredibly generative.
4. Have parties with people who like to debate. Throw out questions that you have been pondering and see what they have to say. Listen to the various perspectives and later take time to reflect on what you heard.
5. Assess the changes going on in the world and see how they affect you now and may affect you in the future. Reflect on what is possible for you and plan your next steps.
6. Put yourself in situations that require you to develop new competencies and to question old ones.

7. Spend time with people who have different styles, approaches, and personalities than your own. Learn how adopting some of their practices or traits might benefit your growth. Learn how to communicate effectively with them and to appreciate your differences. At the least, challenge, if not invalidate, your perceptions.
8. Seek feedback and context frequently.
9. Spend time understanding the meaning that other people ascribe to particular behaviors, words, actions, etc. Try to appreciate their perspectives.
10. Develop a short list of questions you want answers to and/or actions you need to take and get moving.

The Short of it...
Reflection is the pathway to learning and reinvention.

Reflections

Complete the following threads.
1. My favorite time to reflect is...
2. I am most comfortable reflecting when...
3. When I reflect I think about...
4. Reflection impacts me by...
5. The last time I spent time reflecting was.... The focus was.... The result was...
6. The benefits I have gained from engaging in reflection are...

"Unconscious, conflicted, ill-perceived, unaccountable, relationship-challenged, non-reflective leaders are not effective."

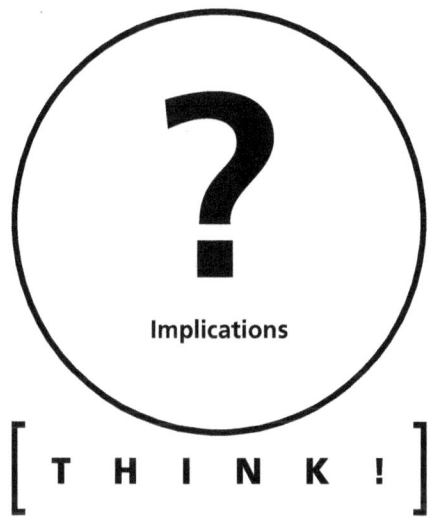

CHAPTER EIGHT

In this chapter, we move from thinking about our personal transformational journeys to how this can also expand our circle of influence in our whole lives. The concepts presented in this book have far reaching implications. Three of the major focal areas in business today are employee engagement, innovation, and leadership effectiveness. The concepts outlined here can have a significant impact on organizational effectiveness in these areas.

Citizen and Employee Engagement

It is important to know and understand that the only real asset any society has is its people. From the hearts and minds of people spring creativity, passion, leadership, productivity, energy, talent and more. If the people are inspired, accountable, connected, communicative, etc., achievement and effectiveness are elevated.

Consciousness is where it begins. If the people are conscious, society will be conscious, for the people make the decisions. And the most conscious group within any society must be leadership. If they are unconscious, they will not be able to engage the people. If people are not engaged in what is going on in their world, the whole society suffers.

This concept is also applicable at the organizational level. Personal brand, or the perception of leaders and managers within the organization, impacts employee engagement. If leaders and managers are not perceived as approachable, open, competent, caring, trustworthy, etc. they will not bear fruit. Effective managers and leaders produce results such as engagement, retention, profitability, growth, productivity, efficiency, innovation and all of the other performance indicators one could list. Now that's some serious fruit!

Simply stated, if the leader is conflicted, not personally aligned, employees will see this, and it poses a barrier to engagement. I have yet to meet an inspiring, conflicted leader. If they hold others accountable but fail to hold themselves to the same standard, they are doomed to ridicule, and their leadership will be resisted. No fruit.

Part of employee engagement is developing and sustaining a relationship founded on mutual trust and respect. If the relationship between leadership, management, and employees does not embody mutual trust and respect, the end result is internal conflict among these constituencies, and the price the organization will pay is employee engagement.

Lastly, an organization that is not engaged in reflection related to its relationship with its employees is likely to become misaligned. Leadership and management may take the position that the employee is a cost center and not an asset and enact policies that erode engagement. Environments characterized by fear and insecurity often fail to bear the fruit of engagement. Employees generally want to be viewed as assets, developed like assets, and treated like assets.

In summary, there is a link between the concepts presented here and employee engagement. Investment in enhancing the ability of leaders and managers to engage employees produces fruit.

Leadership Effectiveness – The Short of it...

Unconscious, conflicted, ill-perceived, unaccountable, relationship-challenged, non-reflective leaders are not effective.

Innovation – The Mini Story

Many companies might as well admit that they don't know exactly what innovation is, but they want some of it! Innovation results from creativity, and creativity comes from people. Employees are able to tap into their creativity and produce innovations in environments that reflect a culture of respect for creativity and innovation.

But what exactly is creativity? Dictionary.com defines creativity as "the ability to transcend traditional ideas, rules, patterns, relationships, or the like, and to create meaningful new ideas, forms, methods, interpretations, etc.; originality, progressiveness, or imagination."

Think about that for a moment. Your most creative employees, those most likely to make innovative breakthroughs that will lead your company to new heights of success, are those who don't always color inside the lines. They are the ones who don't like doing things "the way they've always been done". They are the ones who are most likely to buck the system, to want to do things their way, and to question authority. Employees like that will not stay long in an environment where they are not engaged, where they are constantly criticized, or where they feel that their creativity is stifled.

What if, instead of judging these employees every time they didn't toe the company line, managers and leaders took the time to truly listen to and understand their questions and concerns? What if those employees felt that they had been heard, that management was on their side, that they were valued members of the team with a commitment to goals shared by the entire organization? Imagine what creative employees could accomplish in an environment like that!

The recipe for creating such an environment? Start with five cups of leadership effectiveness. Add 25 cups of management effectiveness. Stir gently. Add 50 cups of employee engagement. Stir to desired consistency. Additional ingredients to be mixed in to your liking include strategy, systems thinking, technology, process infrastructure, strategic alliances and partnerships, capital and any other ingredients you deem necessary for your situation.

Do you notice how just a little effectiveness at the top of an organization goes such a long way? When leaders clearly demonstrate the kinds of attitudes and behaviors they expect, their efforts are multiplied along the command chain. Creating a culture where everyone feels valued and engaged pays off exponentially down the line.

Closing Comments

The chapters of this book are laden with metaphors that relate to theoretical constructs from a vast body of knowledge and research in the areas of communications, leadership, management, organizational behavior, psychology, sociology and the like.

I hope the Traveler's journey has made you think about your personal and professional journey as a parent, spouse, sister, brother, friend, leader, manager, individual contributor, team member or whatever area of your life that came to mind as you followed along. The key point of this book is to convey that we are all Travelers, whether we are conscious of it or not, and the most difficult part of the journey may be from the inside out.

I have applied the techniques outlined by the teachers in my life and have benefited greatly. Along my journey I have encountered many teachers who have invested their time and energy helping me to develop as a person and as a professional. I also have had great role models that model unconditional love and care for others and ask for nothing in return. They give of themselves because it is "their way," and it aligns with the "purpose" they have defined for their lives.

My challenge to you is that you "THINK!" and "Reflect"

on what you have read here and that you take at least one day of the many days remaining in your life to "THINK!" about how to get out of your own way. I wish you the best on your journey.

Reflections

Complete the following threads.
1. My impression of this book is…
2. The stories and concepts in this book caused me to…
3. The benefits I can gain from applying these concepts and practices are…
4. As a result of reading this book, I will be able to improve my ability to…
5. Professionally, this book has helped me to realize…
6. Personally, this book has helped me to realize…
7. I will recommend this book to…
8. I will discuss the concepts in this book with…
9. I will take action by…
10. I expect to change…

BIBLIOGRAPHY

Argyris, C., & Schön, D. *Theory in Practice: Increasing Professional Effectiveness.* San Francisco: Jossey Bass, 1974.

Argyris, Chris. *Reasons and Rationalizations: The Limits to Organizational Knowledge.* Oxford, UK: Oxford University Press, 2004.

Argyris, Chris. "Skilled Incompetence." Harvard Business Review, September-October 1986, pp 74-79.

Badaracco, J.L., Jr. *Defining Moments: When Managers Must Choose Between Right and Right.* Boston, MA: Harvard Business School Press, 1997.

Bean, R., & Radford, R. *The Business of Innovation: Managing the Corporate Imagination for Maximum Results.* New York, NY: AMACOM, 2002.

Branden, Nathaniel. *The Six Pillars of Self-Esteem.* New York, NY: Bantam Books, 1994.

Branden, Nathaniel. *The Psychology of Self-Esteem.* New York, NY: Bantam Books, 1969.

Bridges, William. *Transitions: Making Sense of Life's Changes.* Cambridge, MA: Perseus Books, 1980.

Brookfield, S.D. *Developing Critical Thinkers.* San Francisco, CA: Jossey Bass, 1997.

Collins, J.C. *Good to Great: Why Some Companies Make the Leap... And Others Don't.* New York, NY: Harper Business, 2001.

Covey, S.R. *The Seven Habits of Highly Effective People: Restoring the Character Ethic.* New York, NY: Fireside, 1989.

Cushman, D.P., & Dudley, C.D., Jr.. *Communication in Interpersonal Relationships.* Albany, NY: State University of New York Press, 1985.

Dotlich, D.L., & Cairo, P.C. *Action Coaching: How to Leverage Individual Performance for Company Success.* San Francisco, CA: Jossey Bass, 1999.

Gardner, Howard. *Changing Minds: The Art and Science of Changing Our Own and Other People's Minds.* Boston, MA: Harvard Business School Press, 2004.

Goleman, D., Boyatzis, R., & McKee, A. *Primal Leadership: Learning to Lead With Emotional Intelligence.* Boston, MA: Harvard Business School Press, 2002.

Hamel, Gary. *Leading the Revolution.* Boston, MA: Harvard Business School Press, 2000.

Hesselbein, F., Goldsmith, M., & Somerville, I. *Leading for Innovation and Organizing Results.* San Francisco, CA: Jossey Bass, 2002.

LaFasto, F. & Larson, C. *When Teams Work Best.* Thousand Oaks, CA: Sage Publications, Inc., 2001.

Leeds, D. *The 7 Powers of Questions: Secrets to Successful Communication in Life and at Work.* New York, NY: Berkeley Publishing Group, 2000.

Kets De Vries, M.F.R. *Struggling With the Demon: Perspectives and Organizational Irrationality.* Madison, CT: Psychosocial Press, 2001.

Kets De Vries, M.F.R., & Miller D. *The Neurotic Organization.* San Francisco, CA: Jossey Bass, 1984.

Kinlaw, D.C. *Coaching for Commitment: Interpersonal Strategies for Obtaining Superior Performance from Individuals and Teams.* 2nd Ed. San Francisco, CA: Jossey Bass, 1999.

Kouzes, J.M., & Posner, B.Z. *Credibility: How Leaders Gain and Lose It, Why People Demand It.* San Francisco, CA: Jossey Bass, 1993.

Kouzes, J.M., & Posner, B.Z. *The Leadership Challenge.* San Francisco, CA: Jossey Bass, 1995.

Morgan, Gareth. *Images of Organizations, 2nd ed.* Thousand Oaks, CA: Sage Publications, Inc., 1997.

Oakley, E., Krug, D. *Enlightened Leadership: Getting to the Heart of Change.* New York, NY: Fireside, 1991.

Payne, T. *A Company of One: The Power of Independence in the Workplace.* Albuquerque, NM. Performance Press, 1993.

Prochaska, J.O., Norcross, J.C. & DiClemente, C.C. *Changing for Good.* New York: Morrow, 1994. Released in paperback by Avon, 1995.

Robinson, E.T. *Why Aren't You More Like Me?* Amherst, MA: HRD Press, Inc., 1994.

Seligman, M.E.P. *What You Can Change and What You Can't: The Complete Guide to Successful Self-improvement.* New York: Knopf, 1993.

Senge, P.M. *The Fifth Discipline: The Art and Practice of the Learning Organization.* New York, NY: Currency and Doubleday, 1990.

ABOUT THE AUTHOR

Kevin L. King, Founder & CEO of Transformation Point, Incorporated, is a certified Birkman Method® consultant and management consultant with over thirty years of experience developing leaders, defining solutions to business challenges, improving organizational performance, leading teams, implementing business solutions, and managing strategic organizational change. Kevin has extensive experience working with and for "Big 4" consulting firms delivering strategic engagements and driving transformational change.

His industry experience includes local, state and federal government, healthcare, energy, communications, and manufacturing, and he has held a number of positions including Director, Vice President, Partner and CEO. He has a successful track record in both business and education. With clients all over the world, including China, France, Finland, Germany, Belgium, Spain, Ireland, Italy, and the Czech Republic, Kevin currently coaches executives and management teams in effective strategies to increase individual, team and organizational performance.

Kevin has completed all course work towards a Doctorate in Human Communication Studies at the University of Denver, and has an MBA in Management Information Systems from Oklahoma City University and a BS in Business Administration from Wayland Baptist University. Kevin also attended International Program Management School in France, Systems Dynamics Training through the University of Bergen in Norway, and has completed the Jonah Program at the Goldratt Institute in Theory of Constraints.

A husband, father, grandfather and Air Force veteran., Kevin enjoys spending time with his family, golf, speaking, travel, learning guitar, helping people achieve their potential, and anything related to understanding human dynamics.

www.ingramcontent.com/pod-product-compliance
Lightning Source LLC
Chambersburg PA
CBHW050819160426
43192CB00010B/1822